A CONCISE HISTORY OF
BRANDENBURG—PRUSSIA
TO 1786

Otis C. Mitchell

University Press
of America™

For: Archie Christopherson, Jack Grow,
Gene Goltz, Carroll Kloeker, Don Parker, and
Dallas Wiebe, all of whom would have found
something to interest them in the Tobacco
Parliament.

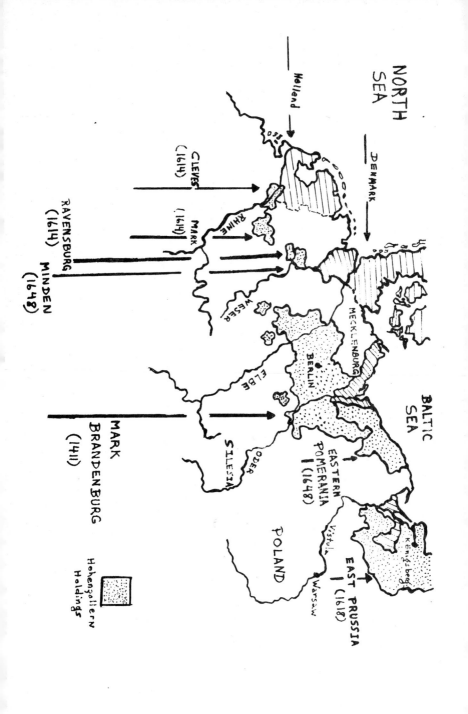

vi

TABLE OF CONTENTS

CHAPTER I

THE ORIGINS OF THE PRUSSIAN STATE

As is the case with so much of German history, an excellent place to begin the history of Prussia is with the reign of the great Frankish emperor--Charlemagne. During his wars to expand the Frankish holdings, Charlemagne pushed the frontiers of his empire eastward to the area of the Elbe River. Having done that, the Emperor of the Franks was content to establish at a number of locations along the Elbe a border count (a Markgraf or Margrave) to defend his domain. One of the most important of these border counts was the man who ruled over the North Mark in the area of the central Elbe valley.

In the year 1134 Albert the Bear of the Ascanian family was given rule over the North Mark by the Holy Roman Emperor. Once installed, Albert quickly saw the advantage to himself of extending his rule eastward from the Elbe and he pushed into the East-Elbian area with his soldiers. Among his first conquests was the old hill fortress of Brandenburg. Once the Brandenburg fortress was taken, a bishopric was established there. From Brandenburg Albert resumed his eastward march. Eventually, he conquered as far as the Oder, extinguishing, driving off, or Christianizing the native Slavic population. In time, most of the indigenous Slavs were absorbed or replaced by Germanic peoples and this domain of Albert's came to be known as Mark Brandenburg.

Albert the Bear, and those who were to rule after him, were involved in nearly constant wars with their neighbors and, through such conflicts, gradually added to the original Mark a whole series of tiny holdings. These territories eventually added up to a kingdom

1

about the size of the state of Vermont.
However, in the fragmented and decentralized
world that was medieval Germany, a territorial
and political unit of this size, coupled with
its geographic location, made the Margraves
of Brandenburg stronger rulers than any of
the German princes of that day other than
the Holy Roman Emperor himself. Moreover,
the strength of the Ascanian Margraves was
enhanced by their function in the empire;
they were in charge of a military outpost
maintained against the enemies of the Holy
Roman Emperor and thus kept under arms what
was, in medieval terms, a large feudal fighting
force for that purpose. Given the kind of
power he had achieved, it was only natural
that, by the year 1230, the ruler of Brandenburg came to be accepted by the other German
princes as one of the seven men who had the
right to elect the German emperor.

The Brandenburg Ascanians died out
in 1320 and Mark Brandenburg passed into the
hands of the Wittelsbach family, rulers of
Bavaria in southern Germany, who actually
had very little time for their new holding.
Thereafter, Brandenburg passed into the hands
of the Holy Roman Emperor who finally passed
it on, for military services rendered, to
Frederick I of Hohenzollern who was made
Elector of Brandenburg in 1417. From that
time forward Mark Brandenburg remained under
the control of the Hohenzollern family, a
dynasty which was to become one of the most
famous in Europe.

Subsequent Hohenzollern rulers fought
the kind of battles that almost all medieval
princes had to fight to maintain and further
centralize their power. A case in point is
the career of Hohenzollern elector Frederick II
(ruled 1440-1470). Frederick II was known
with good cause as "Iron Tooth."

2

Frederick II was sorely vexed by the independence and pretensions displayed by the aldermen who ruled the towns of Mark Brandenburg. These towns were fortified and self-governing. They claimed and exercised wide economic and judicial privileges. Moreover, they banded together in leagues to ensure the perpetuation of their prerogatives.

Iron Tooth's chance against the towns came in 1442. A quarrel broke out in Berlin between the patricians who ran the city and the disfranchised lower social classes. Frederick entered the city with an armed force. Under threat of considerable physical harm, he made the city councilers give over the keys of the city to him. The city council was dissolved and replaced by instruments of the Elector's own devising. Six months later Iron Tooth abolished the local aldermens' right to choose their own judges and forced them to cede to the government of the Electorate a plot of ground near the center of town on an island formed by the branching of the Spree River. On this site he built a fortress designed to force the local citizenry to obey him. The literal translation of this building's title reveals its purpose; it was known as the "Coercion Castle" (the *Zwingburg*). The Hohenzollern castle which grew from this original building was to remain standing for the next 500-plus years.

From this time forward, living in the midst of its citizens, Iron Tooth made Berlin the political capital of Brandenburg. Moreover, his location there enabled him to quell instantly any revolt of his subjects living in the city. And there were revolts as soon as the Hohenzollern Coercion Castle began to rise out of the ground. In 1448 the local inhabitants of Berlin, unable to stand the affront to their independence that they saw in the Zwingburg, opened a sluice to the River Spree in an attempt to flood the new

building's foundations. They then stormed
the palace itself, forced open its doors,
and ran wildly through its halls. They
arrested the judge Iron Tooth had appointed
and held him hostage. Then they sent messages
to Iron Tooth indicating that they would not
release the captured official until the independence of their city had been restored by
the Hohenzollern Elector.

Having made these initial giant steps
along the rebellious path, the Berlin insur-
rectionaries sought to gain support from the
other towns in Mark Brandenburg. Messages
were sent out to these other communities
carrying the sentiment that Iron Tooth was
a tyrant who ran roughshod over the traditional
civic rights of towns even as he restricted
personal freedoms. As it turned out, however,
only three or four other towns had the courage
to join the Berliners in their rebellion.
Soon enough, Frederick Iron Tooth of Hohenzollern
has surrounded Berlin with 6,000 armed knights
ready to crush the rebellion. Faced with
such unfavorable odds the inhabitants of the
city currendered.

By 1452, Frederick had broken the
resistance of the towns. Iron Tooth spend
his later years adding with patience and care
more lands to the Electorate than would any
of his successors for the next 200 years.
His major additions came from the profiting
by the distress, more precisely the lack of
funds, of the Teutonic Knights (a quasi-
religious order originating in the Crusades
of which more is to be said later) by purchas-
ing from them much valuable land to the east
or the older Brandenburgian territories.
Thereafter, these added territories were known
as the New Mark.

Frederick also made war on a regular
basis against Pomerania to the north. Finally,
while directing the seige of Uckermünde,

Frederick was dining between actions when
a cannonball crashed through the window of
his room and through a table in front of him;
for the Elector lived in an era when gunpowder
had begun to shape the art of making war in
Europe. This particular gunpowder-related
incident destroyed the Elector's hearing and
impaired his memory. By nature a pious and
melancholy man, he soon resigned the Electorate
into the keeping of his brother, Albert
Achilles (1470-1486), and retired to a castle
in Franconia where he died the following year.
During his reign, Albert Achilles, whose name
"Achilles" was added to the original Albert
because of his great strength and warlike
nature, completed the subjugation of the towns
within the Mark.

        The activities of the early Hohenzollern
Rulers, monarchs like Frederick Iron Tooth
and Albert Achilles, have caused some historians
to berate them as "the most backward and
despised of all the Electors." This judgment
is a bit harsh. The Hohenzollerns came to
control Brandenburg at a time when centralized
authority had almost completely broken down
in Germany. The Holy Roman Empire was not
a state in the modern sense but rather a loose
confederation of territories over which the
Emperor presided as, at best, a first among
equals. Moreover, even within smaller territorial units like Mark Brandenburg the towns
and/or Leagues of Knights, etc. were constantly
rebelling against the authority of the local
ruler. Often violent military action was
the most obvious way to deal with this problem.
The Hohenzollerns simply turned out to be
better at dealing with this vexing quandry
than most of the other princes of Germany
who also faced it.

* * * * * * * *

At the end of the Middle Ages and on the even of the Protestant Reformation in Germany the ruler of Mark Brandenburg was the Hohenzollern prince Joachim I (1499-1535). Joachim was in many ways a typical Hohenzollern; he did not hesitate to use force to ensure the perpetuation of his family's unhampered control over the territories within the Mark. Inside the first two years of his reign he had had some forty robber-nobles decapitated or hanged. In this era of history the kind of violence just described often ran as a concurrent strain through the personalities of men as a close companion to extreme piety, a tendency which also flourished there. Not just small dashes of intolerance and superstition were often added as well. Joachim I was no exception as the following examples should serve to indicate.

Joachim I was a passionately orthodox Roman Catholic. Although hardly very circumspect in his own morality (ke kept many mistresses), he did make genuine effots to raise some of the clergy from the low state of immorality and general ignorance into which they had fallen. Joachim was, as a profoundly devoted Catholic, horrified by the advent of the Protestant Reformation. When he discovered that his wife, Elizabeth of Denmark, was a secret Protestant, he threatened to imprison his mate for the rest of her life. Unwilling to wait around to see if Joachim would actually make good on his threat, Elizabeth fled Berlin, making her escape by night in the company of only one maid and one groom. Eventually, Elizabeth found shelter in neighboring Saxony where she remained.

Joachim's superstition, as indicated, was equally as great as his intolerance. Joachim was interested in learning, although his greatest fascination was with the more dubious disciplines like astrology. It was his fascination with areas like astrology

6

which led Joachim in 1506 to found the first
university in the Electorate at Frankfurt
on the Oder. His passion for astrology also
caused him to have a small observatory built
into his palace. With observations made from
this location, the court astrologers managed
to predict that all of the Mark Brandenburg
would be destroyed by a flood on July 15,
1525. Joachim, a prudent and cautious man,
decided he would make ready for the coming
inundation. At the very least, he meant to
rescue his court. There was little time in
which to construct an ark in the manner of
Noah. Instead, the Elector quickly herded
his court onto a wagon train and then made
for the Kreuzberg, the highest point in the
region. Unfortunately, unlike Mount Ararat
of Biblical fame where Noah's ark is supposed
to have settled after the great flood, which
pierced the clouds at 14,000 feet, the
Kreuzberg was only 217 feet high.

Joachim felt confirmed in his dire
forecasts when it indeed began to rain on
those assembled there atop the Kreuzberg.
The Elector and his court sat on top the hill
all afternoon while a drizzle soaked them
to the bone. Soldiers stood waiting on the
lower slope of Joachim's elevated refuge ready
to stop any of the common folk who, in panic
at the coming flood, tried to reach the higher
ground already held by the ruler and his court.
Presumably, commoners with any sense at all
stayed at home and kept dry under their
thatched roofs.

Eventually, of course, the rain stopped
and there was no flood. Sheepish nobles waded
through the mud to reach their carriages while
crowds of the local people came to watch the
spectacle. Although this scene may appear
ridiculous by modern standards, one must keep
in mind the spirit of the times. It was
Martin Luther, Joachim's contemporary, who
believed that Prussia was infested "by devils"

and that Lapland was full "of witches."
Moreover, in spite of his eccentricities,
and in spite of the fact that he was in many
ways an irresolute weakling, Joachim did
manage to see the influence of the house of
Hohenzollern extended during his reign.

During the days of Joachim I, his cousin
Albert was elected Grand Master of the Tuetonic
Order (1511). Albert eventually transformed
the territory of the Order into a hereditary
territory belonging to the Hohenzollern family
(1525) and it was inherited by the Electors
themselves in 1618. In 1513, Joachim's younger
brother, another Albert, became Bishop of
Halberstadt and Archbishop of Magdeburg. In
the next year Albert became Archbishop of
Mainz. In this way the Honenzollerns came
to hold two of the seven seats on the Electoral
College, the body responsible for picking
the Holy Roman Emperor during the crucial
years of the Reformation. Eventually, the
sees of Halberstadt and Magdeburg were incor-
porated into randenburg-Prussia (in 1648 and
1680). Thus was the Prussian state built,
bit by bit and piece by piece over a very
long period of time.

During his life, Joachim I remained
a determined foe of Lutheranism. On his death,
however, his son, Joachim II (1535-1571),
took his place on the throne only to be implored
immediately by both religious parties in the
Reformation controversy to join their cause.
For four years Joachim II, who had talked
with Martin Luther early during his years
and who had a secret inclination toward
Lutheranism, refused to move to one side or
the other. But it is difficult to be a fence-
straddler forever. Eventually, the majority
of his subjects began to clamor for a move
tow:\rd Lutheranism. Joachim II gave in. On
November 1, 1539, the Elector of Brandenburg
took part openly in Lutheran ceremonies for
the first time. Before his reign had ended,

Joachim II had adopted Lutheranism as his personal faith and Brandenburg went down the Protestant road with most of the other states in the north German lands.

* * * * * * * *

At this point, it is time to leave the history of the Hohenzollern electors momentarily to move to another important influence shaping the history of Brandenburg-Prussia--the Teutonic Knights. We have already seen how a Hohenzollern took the lands of that order for his own house in 1525. Before that happened, however, the Teutonic Order had set something of a permanent stamp on the character of the Prussian nobility, a lasting seal both warlike and chivalric. It is to an inspection of the military-monastic order called "Teutonic" that we now turn.

East Prussia resembles Brandenburg topographically. The land was one of sandy plains, lakes, and small watercourses. It had a long seacoast on the Baltic. But this area was colonized by a religio-military order instead of by secular princes as Brandenburg had been. The native population was more Slavic than German and it is from this native population that the term "Prussian" derives. For approximately 1,000 years before the thirteenth century the native Slavic Prussians had lived in the area of the East Baltic coast. Periodically, there had been border conflicts between these people and the Poles. The agents of the Polish kingdom often tried to conquer and/or Christianize the Prussians. Finally, in the year 1226, a Polish Prince, Conrad of Mazovia, unable to handle the Prussians militarily, called in the Teutonic Knights to help him.

The Teutonic Knights (the Deutschritter Orden) had initially developed during the

Third Crusade. The Knights, like other similar
orders, were modeled on the Knights Templar,
originally recruited by St. Bernard of Clairvaux.
That holy man had called out for warriors:
"gentler than lambs and fiercer than lions,
wedding the mildness of the monk to the valour
of the knight, so that it is difficult to
tell what to call them: men who adorn the
Temple of Solomon with weapons instead of
gems. . . ."

These early monastic-military orders
founded on a base of high idealism were on
the wane by the end of the twelfth century.
St. Bernard's original idea of a rigidly dis-
ciplined body of men, dedicated to the service
of Christ, sworm to a simultaneous service
to the New Testament and the sword, had been
suberted. Too many restless knights-errant,
living only for excitement, had lost the
original purpose of the Templars while pursuing
a simple quest for adventure and gold. Consequently, the early monastic purity was nearly
extinct by about the year 1200. It was
precisely at that point, however, that a new
order of this military-monastic sort made
its appearance in 1190 and came to be called
the "Tuetonic Knights."

This new knightly order appeared during
the Third Crusade's darker hours. Disease
was rampant in the army of crusaders, German
knights for the most part, who were camped
outside the city of Acre. Merchants from
Bremen and Lübeck took pity on their helpless
countrymen and spread the sails of their ships
to make tents to shelter the sick. They also
provided beds, hospital equipment, and the
finances to maintain what they had provided.
Eventually, once the city of Jerusalem was
conquered, a German merchant obtained the
grant of a plot of land from King Guy, the
crusader ruler of Jerusalem, to create a
permanent home for his hospital. The hospital
was then given into the care of a chaplain

in October of 1190.   In time the new association
became a knightly-monastic order by confirmation
of Pope Innocent in 1199.

The Teutonic Knights never distinguished
themselves in the Holy Land; these "monks
of war" fought no famous battles there and
did not enjoy any of the abundant wealth which
had helped to corrupt older orders like the
Templars.   This German order of monastic
knights was therefore happy enough to accept
the invitation of Conrad of Mazovia to return
from the Holy Land in order to launch a crusade
against the heathen Prussians.   The offer
to participate in the anti-Prussian crusade
was sweetened by the tendering of full sovereignty over any lands they might conquer outside
the Holy Roman Empire.

The heathen Prussians who had lived
so long in the area the Teutonic Knights were
coming to conquer had already been subjected
to earlier attempts at many attributes--their
drinking to excess, their devotion to various
pagan shrines, their less-than-appealing custom
that a widow should not survive the death
of her husband, and the practices of burning
the body of a deceased warrior along with
his living hunting dogs, hunting birds, and
his slaves--which the Church profoundly disliked.

The Tuetonic Order that came to conquer
these heathens was something of an anachronism.
It had appeared and was becoming prominent
in a period when the institutions of medieval
knighthood were already on the wane.   Nevertheless, the knights transferred their forces
from the Holy Land to North Germany so that
they could create a state of their own.   In
1226, therefore, the conquest began.   The
Order of the Teutonic Knights sailed down
the Vistula establishing outposts along the
way.   For the next quarter-century they pushed
through the sands and forests to the east.   In

1255 they founded the city of Königsberg.
In 1261 the native Prussians revolted against
their overlordship and the revolt lasted for
twenty years.

The uprising marked a turning point
in the attitude of the Knights toward the
natives. Where before they had worked out
treaties and ended disagreements between feuding
tribes by acting as arbiters, they were now
sufficiently angered to demand complete submission of the Prussian tribes to their will.
The Prussians were then forced to give up
their native language and made to speak German.
By the end of the thirteenth century, the
Teutonic Order had made itself true master
of much of the eastern Baltic shore. By 1309,
the Knights had established a permanent head-
quarters on the Vistula, a magnificent castle
at Marienburg on the Nogat.

For the next century the Teutonic Knights
flourished. Young nobles from all over Europe
sought to serve in their ranks. As they conquered and opened up eastern lands they brought
in German peasants to settle there. New
popularity came to an old song known in north-
western Germany: "To the Eastland we want
to go, There is a better life." Soon the
influx of German settlers resulted in the
founding of new towns and a flourishing trade
was opened on the Baltic. As time went on
the Knights became more prosperous and conquered
more territory.

Unfortunately for the continued existence
of a prosperous territory ruled over by the
Order a gulf widened between the Knights and
the German settlers. The Knights were always
a narrow oligarchy ruled over by some 400-
odd nobles from Germany. Their tendency was
to control monopolistically commercial activities
in their area through unfair tariff laws or
exclusive control of profitable trading items.
As the Knights came to be increasingly resented,

great currency was given to rumors that they
cared far more for indulging themselves in
their wealth at sumptuous and noisy banquets
than attending to their religious duties.
It was widely circulated that they had turned
their backs on their original monastic vows
of silence in favor of talk about horses,
women, and the telling of off-color stories.
Indeed, it appeared that prosperity was taking
the German religio-military order in the same
direction that affluence had taken the Templars
before them, toward moral corruption.

In time the Poles came to regret that
they had originally helped in forming this
Germanic state along the Baltic. Border clashes
between the Poles and the Order increased
in number. In 1409 Poland declared war.

The conflict with Poland marks the
beginning of a century of decline and decay
for the eutonic Knights. In 1410 they engaged
the Poles at the Battle of Tannenburg. Out-
numbered two to one, the best of the Order
was destroyed. By 1453, the Prussian nobles
and towns formed an alliance against the once-
powerful Knights. The Poles intervened gladly.
After thirteen years of fighting, the Order
had lost West Prussia to Poland. The Knights
retained only East Prussia, and that only
as a fief from the Polish ruler.

It was because the Knights were so
weakened in their struggle with the Poles
that they sought to reinvigorate themselves
by choosing leaders from among the sons of
the powerful territorial princes in Germany.
It was this sort of aim that was the most
important motive behind their picking Albert
of Hohenzollern as Grandmaster in 1511. It
was Albert, as mentioned earlier, who finally
dissolved the Order and transformed its holdings into a duchy, a duchy which eventually
became part of Brandenburg-Prussia. By the
time of the Order's decline, however, its

role in history had been to open the Baltic
to considerable Germanic settlement. Because
of the activities of the Order, the foundations
of the later Brandenburg-Prussian kingdom
had been set in the east.

* * * * * * * *

Those rulers who succeeded Joachim II
in Brandenburg, the men who ruled from 1571
to 1608, contributed little to the further
development of the Hohenzollern state. It
was during the reign of John Sigismund (1608-
1619) that the next important acquisition
of territory occurred. When Albert Frederick,
Duke of Prussia, died in 1618 the Elector
of Brandenburg became, simultaneously, Duke
of Prussia. From the date of this inheritance
the state of Brandenburg-Prussia can be said
to exist. Earlier in the reign of John
Sigismund (1614) the Elector had taken over
the administration of Cleves, Mark, and Ravens-
burg in the west, small islands of territories
in the Rhineland. The Hohenzollerns thus
ruled over lands which were scattered all
the way from Poland to the Rhineland. Indeed,
some of their holdings were so widely separated
for so long a period of time that historians
have referred to the phenomenon of these spread-
out holdings as "The Scattered Frontier of
Brandenburg-Prussia." The union of the lands
was only a personal one. Each time that a
Hohenzollern ruler wished to travel from one
to another of his possessions he had to pass
through someone else's lands. It is little
wonder that later rulers of Prussia developed
a strong desire to obtain those areas between
the scattered wings of Prussia. Before that
could be done, however, German lands were
to be ravaged by the Thirty Years' War. Hardly
had John Sigismund united the three sections
of Brandenburg-Prussian lands when the German

states entered upon one of the most terrible
wars of all history.

* * * * * * * *

The Thirty Year's War had just begun
when John Sigismund died and was succeeded
by his son, George William (1619-1640). The
new ruler was a weak one, certainly not the
kind of monarch needed at a time of such severe
threat to the state by foreign enemies; for
Brandenburg was nearly indefensible, since
not a single city in it was much more than
a day's march from the frontier. The economic
situation of the Hohenzollerns' state was
such that most of the local estates controlled
their own revenues. Thus, George William
had almost no available money with which to
hire mercenary soldiers. This was at a time
in history when most armies still consisted
of those professionals whose only loyalty
was to the highest bidder; for the modern
national standing army had not yet really
developed. As a consequence, much of the
Hohenzollern lands were reduced to ashes.
Large portions of the population sank to a
state of barbarism. There were great famines.
In one place starvation was so extensive that
the chroniclers tell us in horror that "men
ate human flesh" and in extreme instances
"human creatures ate their own children."

George William, the hapless Elector
ruling in the midst of all this, although
himself a Calvinist by persuasion, kept switching sides in what was basically a religio-
political conflict. He tried neutrality.
He had recourse to an alliance with the Lutheran
Swedes. And he attempted an alliance with
the Catholic forces of the Austrian Holy Roman
Emperor. Each new combination he selected
seemed to have worse consequences for his
state than the one immediately preceding it.
The result always seemed to be more misery

15

and greater misfortune for his subjects.
Thomas Carlyle, the famous English historian,
has written of George William that: "George
William did what is to be called nothing in
the Thirty Years' War; his function was only
that of suffering."

In sum, the Thirty Years' War was far
worse than most conflicts. Rival forces raged
back and forth through towns and across farm-
lands. As they went, they ravaged and
pillaged. Torture was common and religious
reasons for it were often given, although
the motives were commonly unclear. Since
the soldiers were mercenaries, they lived
off the land and took their rewards from sacked
cities. Many agricultural areas stopped pro-
ducing completely and both soldiers and peasants
commenced to starve. Dead men were found
with grass in their mouths. Jailers ate the
flesh of their prisoners. The plague spread.
Some German towns almost ceased to exist.
Magdeburg lost 90 percent of its population.
Berlin was reduced to one-half. Perhaps the
spirit of the times is best revealed to us
by contemporary woodcuts which portray trees
festooned with hanging bodies.

By 1638, George William had had enough.
Suffering from an old wound in his leg he
was taken from Berlin to Königsberg where
he thought he would be safer. Behind him
he left in charge Adam von Schwartzenberg,
a strong-minded man who tended to be loyal
to the Austrian camp, to the Catholic Habsburgs.
Actually, he very likely received secret bribes
from Vienna. Schwartzenberg then became virtual
dictator. But Schwartzenberg's death cut
short his rule in all but name over the Brandenburg
Prussian state on March 14, 1641. Only a
short time earlier George William had also
died and had been succeeded by his son,
Frederick William, an inexperienced youth
of only twenty years. The fortunes of the

kingdom were about to change radically, although any person living at that time would hardly have thought so.

CHAPTER II

THE RULE OF THE GREAT ELECTOR

On the death of Elector George William (December 1, 1640) the Electorate passed to his only son. The heir to the throne had been born in the castle at Berlin on February 16, 1620, less than two years after the outbreak of the Thirty Years' War. From nearly his initial breath Frederick William was troubled by this terrible war; for some months he lay unbaptized in his cradle. No money for the expected baptismal services could be found. At the age of seven, when the Electorate was under the threat of the Austrian emperor's armies, Frederick William was removed from Berlin to the fortress of Küstrin. There he was placed under the care of a tutor who coached him in various subjects. Of greatest importance, his teacher imparted to his pupil an attitude of deep Calvinist religious devotion. At Küstrin Frederick William also learned to ride, hunt, shoot, and fence. All of these skills were indispensable to the education of a gentleman-prince. At twelve he shot his first deer, and in later life became famous for his skill in the hunt. He also studied mathematics and geography, subjects in which he did only average work. Importantly, he managed during his studies to lay the foundation of a fair command of Latin, Polish, Dutch, and French. Languages such as these would later prove to be invaluable to him in cultivating European-wide contacts.

While Brandenburg was still in the thick of the war, Frederick William was sent to Holland, partly for a stimulating education, partly to ensure his safety. The house of Hohenzollern was so impoverished that the young prince's mother had to cut back on food to pay for the journey. Nevertheless, Frederick William made it to the University of Leyden where he listened to lectures on mechanics and physics. He also became more proficient in languages and sciences even as he became more deeply interested in how commerce could be developed effectively.

Frederick William while in the Netherlands was a guest in the house of Frederick Henry of Orange, a relative of the Hohenzollerns. At this time Frederick Henry of Orange was continuing a Dutch fight for political and religious independence against the Spaniards. At the Orange's camp Frederick William received practical instruction in the art of war. He wrote long letters to his father describing the campaigns of the most able military commander of the era. The letters apparently had little positive impact on his father, but they do serve to reveal the early development on the part of Frederick William of a keen insight into the workings of the military.

There is also an account that remains from about this same time that shows us something of the self-discipline of the man who would one day rule Brandenburg-Prussia. While Frederick William was involved in his military studies, a group of Dutch nobles known as the "Midnight Society" invited him to a late-night meeting of their club. The young prince was warned before he went that the nobles involved in that organization were sybarites and would likely be involved in an orgy by the time he arrived. But Frederick wanted to see for himself if the rumors about the Midnight Society were true. He thus went to the appointed place and, sure enough, an orgy was in progress. Frederick William walked in and looked around. One can only imagine was was passing through his Calvinist-oriented mind. What we do know is that he simply walked in and then back out again. When some of the participants tried to draw him back into the midst of their activities, he refused. He made his way back to Frederick Henry's camp where he told his great-uncle what he had seen. Frederick Henry was greatly pleased that such a young man could tear himself away from the temptations proffered by the Midnight Society. He told his young relative that any person who could learn so much about self-control so early was destined "for something great."

It was not only war, commerce, and self-restraint that the heir to Brandenburg-Prussia learned at the court of the Oranges. In their company he had many chances to talk to the leading statesmen of his day. He had conversations with John Maurice of Nassau, who had been responsible for organizing a colony in Brazil. He had an opportunity to see many new agricultural methods. These methods were greatly advanced over anything done in his own lands as were the Dutch procedures for shipbuilding, their trade, their canals, their art and architecture, and the general level of their culture. All that he had observed stirred high ambitions for what his own domain could become once it was rid of the terrors of the Thirty Years' War.

What Frderick William eventually accomplished was nothing short of astounding. He came to the throne at the age of twenty in 1640 to find a land so ravaged by war as to be nearly destroyed. Moreover, Schwartzenberg, jealous of his own powers, had persuaded the old Elector to shut Frederick William out of the affairs of state. On his return from Holland he was told to stay at Köningsberg where he remained inactive for the two years before his father died. Because of this situation, Frederick William became the Elector without practical experience in governing and faced immediately a situation wherein half the population of the old Mark Brandenburg had been taken by war, murder, famine, and suicide. Fields were no longer cultivated. Roads were impassable. Counterfeit coins were to be found everywhere. Much of his land was occupied by the Swedes. Even his own palace roof was in danger of collapsing and it was some time before he could enter the *Residenzstadt* of Brandenburg-Prussia's ruler, Berlin, and live there in a normal fashion.

The first important order of business for Frederick William was to recognize just how weak he actually was. Once he had done that, he began to place effective councilors in positions of importance. When Schwartzenberg died, the Elector forced the hated minister's men out of the Privy Council and installed his own friends.

To secure the good will of the Polish ruler, who was his feudal overlord in East Prussia, he made a trip to Warsaw to kneel before the King and be invested with the Duchy of East Prussia. He also secured the homage of his Prussian nobles by indicating that he would protect their traditional privileges.

Another early order of business was to rid Brandenburg of troops Schwartzenberg had hired so that the former minister could enter an alliance with the Emperor of Austria once George William had decided in 1638 to leave his subjects in the lurch. The troops Schwartzenberg had recruited were among the worst thugs in Europe. Now that their original master was no longer around these ruffians did not wish to obey the new Elector. One mercenary colonel even demonstrated his disdain for the young prince by threatening Frederick William's subjects in Spandau. There the colonel defiantly threatened to blow up the local fortress and burn the town he had been paid to defend unless he was given a proper ransom. Frederick had no choice but to move against these unruly professional soldiers.

Frederick Williams' lieutenants went
to work. Some of the mercenaries were arrested
and others fled. By the time he was finished
purging his own scum-ridden armies, only about
2,500 troops were left to him. Between that
time and the end of the war he gradually increased
his forces to 8,000 men, decently uniformed
and obedient troops.

In the short term, however, with only
2,500 troops, Frederick William had to have
peace before he could reconstruct his kingdom.
In 1641, he concluded a treaty with the Swedes,
an armistice made possible as a result of
his having excluded those who favored the
forces of the Empire from influence in his
lands. The peace with the Swedes was also
urged upon that northern kingdom by the fact
that the peasants of Brandenburg had risen
against the Swedish troops who had themselves
committed great barbarities. By 1643, Frederick
William was able too establish his residence
in Berlin.

When Frederick William returned to live
permanently in Berlin, he found a city where
the people had fallen back to the worst levels
of barbarism. Many of them were eating dogs,
cats, and rats to stay alive. Some of them
were even devouring the flesh of human dead.
Moreover, it was difficult to get food from
the lands outside the city for his people
because robber barons and the debased elements
of mercenary armies still roamed the land.
Hence, a breathing spell to rebuild the country
and outside help to expedite that process
were badly needed. One way to have secured
outside help and possibly add Pomerania to
his lands, since it was held by the Swedes,
would have been for Frederick William to become
the husband of his cousin, Queen Christina
of Sweden. He secretly explored this possibility. However, court circles in Sweden,
as well as the King of Poland, opposed the
idea. The liaison was made impossible when
it became apparent that Christina herself,

like Elizabeth I of England during the previous century, had no intention of tying herself to a husband and even referred to the Hohenzollern ruler somewhat contemptuously as that "little Burgomaster."

Rebuffed by Sweden, Frederick William finally sought an alliance with the more reliable Dutch house of Orange. On personal grounds, it turned out to be a much better match anyway. Louise Henrietta, daughter of Frederick Henry, became a loving companion for the Elector. And as was not the case in very many arranged monarchical marriages, the young couple really seemed to come to care for each other. Until her death in 1667, Henrietta appeared to act as a modifying influence on Frederick William who, like most of the Hohenzollerns, was given to sudden bursts of anger and ruling with a very heavy hand. One last aspect of this Dutch marriage was also important; it led to the idea of repopulating the ravaged lands of Brandenburg with Dutchmen who were brought in by such inducements as tax-free status, free lumber from the royal forests, etc.

As might be expected, many of the local German peasants resented the favored treatment given to what seemed to them to be overly privileged Dutch interlopers. Frederick William moved quickly to soothe their injured feelings. He rented out many of his private fisheries and vineyards to local subjects. He removed oppressive duty payments. Meanwhile, he continued to build up the standing army.

A standing army was something of a novelty in those days of mercenary soldiers. The fighting men of Brandenburg-Prussia were under the Elector's command personally. Most nobles in the realm opposed this army as a direct threat to their independence. But the Elector went ahead and built it up anyway. And it was that standing army of some 8,000 men

which gave him such a strong negotiating
position in the long peace talks at Münster
and Osnabrück in Westphalia (1644 to 1648)
aimed at ending the Thirty Years' War.

Frederick William was the champion
of the Calvinist cause in these negotiations,
attempting to ensure his co-religionists rights
on an equal footing with the Lutherans and
the Catholics. This he accomplished by the
religious portions of the Treaty of Westphalia.
He also attempted at the treaty tables to
obtain the whole of Pomerania for Prussia,
thus extracting the Swedes from North German
affairs. In this he was not so successful.

To compensate Frederick William for
his disappointment at not obtaining all of
Pomerania, the Westphalian conference gave
him Eastern Pomerania and several bishoprics,
one of which (Minden on the Weser) served
as a stepping stone between Brandenburg and
the Western possessions of Brandenburg-Prussia.

* * * * * * *

After the end of the Thirty Years'
War, there were seven years of peace. Frederick
William used these years to carry forward
some of his internal reforms. Many of these
were extensions of those mentioned earlier.
Much of his time was also involved in asserting
his rights over ducal Prussia and crushing
the power of the nobles there. Naturally enough,
he was charged by some of these nobles as
being ruthless and unscrupulous. But Frederick
William was not a royal extremist. He was
well within the models of absolutism developing
during his age. He was motivated by one basic
drive; he wanted to make the most he could
out of Brandenburg-Prussia.

Frederick William was interrupted in
his internal projects by war between his

neighbors Poland and Sweden in 1655. The new international conflict had its origins in the fact that Queen Christina of Sweden decided to abdicate her throne. She had long enjoyed shocking Europe by wearing masculine clothes and riding to the hunt in the manner of a man. Now she provided the ultimate shock; she turned her back on Lutheranism and became a Roman Catholic. She left Sweden soon thereafter to spend the rest of her picturesque life in Rome.

The major importance, beyond its merely colorful aspects, of Queen Christina's leavetaking was that the throne of Sweden passed to her cousin Charles. And Charles was a very warlike man. Sweden was troubled as was the case in so many countries after the Thirty Years' War by a disorderly soldiery which had long since lost all sense of mercy and had become a plague upon the land. Charles' idea was to get their soldiers out of the country through the expedient of a foreign war. Eventually, he decided to attack Poland where he had dynastic claims to the throne. He moved against the Polish forces in 1655, his plan being to turn the Baltic into a Swedish pond. Suddenly, Frederick William was faced with a war along his borders, a clash between nations that might well spill over into his own lands.

This "Northern War," as it came to be called, caused Frederick William, at one point or another, to pursue three separate courses: (1) neutrality; (2) to side with Sweden; and (3) to assist Poland. His various moves in solution to this quandry seem, at least to some extent, to justify Thomas Carlyle's later assessment of him that he was one "of the shiftiest of men." What Frederick did was to adopt a policy of opportunism and follow, at one time or another, all three of the courses listed above. The

26

end result of this tortuous policy was a positive one for Brandenburg-Prussia. The demeaning feudal overlordship Poland had exercised over the Elector and the predecessors in Prussia since 1466 was at an end. Moreover, the Swedes had been forced into a position of lesser importance in North German affairs. One negative outcome was the fact that, even given lesser Swedish importance, it was still necessary to cede Upper Pomerania to Sweden.

* * * * * * * *

To pursue the role he had followed in the North War, Frederick William found it necessary to increase taxes. Increased taxes meant it was necessary for the Elector to further centralize the institutions of his government. The Northern War, even more than the Thirty Years' War, had led to the establishment of greater royal absolutism at the expense of the medieval-style estates. And the nobles who constituted these estates resented that fact. Moreover, the estates had believed that they would be called together regularly for consultation before they granted any more monies to their ruler. The Brandenburg nobles had been led to believe that, after they granted 530,000 taler in 1653, to be paid over six years, to help provide for the common defense, they would be called again six years later to discuss the Elector's monetary needs for the operation of the state. But 1659 fell during the campaigns of the Northern War. Consequently, Frederick William still collected the taxes he had collected since 1653 and the estates were not called to provide their approval. Thereafter, the would-be Diet of Estates grumbled but did not meet again. Instead, Frederick William worked with a hand-picked committee to manage the financial machinery. Frederick William also transformed various local officials into instruments of royal authority.

The end result of policies like the ones just mentioned was the establishment in Brandenburg-Prussia of royal absolutism. Thereafter, absolutism in the state was based on: (1) an enlarged standing army; (2) new taxes to support that army; and (3) new officials to bring the authority of the central government to both rural areas and urban centers.

Naturally enough, given their long-standing feudal privileges, the lords and nobles who made up the estates of Frederick William's various domains resented this detraction from their power. They resented officials from the central government taking over such tasks as the administration of entire towns in the name of the Elector. Such towns had enjoyed self-government since the Middle Ages. It was not unexpected that there would be some resistance.

The most successful resistance on the part of the estates was to be seen in Cleves-Mark. These estates were far removed from the nerve center of Frederick William's kingdom in Berlin. Moreover, Cleves-Mark received some backing for their stance of greater autonomy from the Dutch, despite that dynasty's close familial relationship with Frederick William. Frederick William felt it necessary first to grant some of the demands of the Cleves-Mark estates. For example, he exempted them from taxation, indicated that he would not build fortresses for defense in their territories, and other similar privileges. After the Northern War, however, he took a firmer stand. The Elector established some garrisons at that time in Cleves-Mark. And he worked out a bargain whereby, even though the local inhabitants were exempt from taxes, they did provide regular and generous grants to aid in the maintaining of the army.

An extended conflict with the local nobles over who was to control their destinies

transpired in East Prussia. There, during
over two centuries of time, the estates had
acquired enormous privileges. Initially,
feudal prerogatives had been concessions
granting greater independence which had been
forced from the Grandmaster of the Teutonic
Order and, after 1525, from the Hohenzollerns.
The nobles in this area talked of "liberties."
What these liberties meant were far from modern
individual civil rights. Rather, the refer-
ence was to the right to do exactly as one
wished on one's own lands, the unbridled
license to persecute one's underlings, use
funds as one desired, and to appeal to the
Polish King as overlord if troubled. Frederick
William, once the Northern War had ended,
discovered that negotiations and discussions
did not work with the nobles in his East
Prussian domains who were so used to being
virtually independent of royal control. Having
recently secured in the war Poland's agreement
to his full sovereignty in the area, Frederick
William was able to bring 2,000 troops to
Köningsberg (1662) to enforce his authority
without Polish interference. At that time
he imprisoned some of his rebellious leaders.
Later (in 1669) the same estates refused for
months to grant requested taxes. When this
initial recalcitrance sparked further rebellion,
Frederick brought some of the rebellious leaders
down and imprisoned them. When rebellion
was a continuing phenomenon, he became more
severe, torturing and executing some of the
leaders of the resistance. After his display
of severity, there was further little trouble
from the Prussian nobility.

* * * * * * * *

The period after the end of the Northern
War (1660 onto the end of the century) reminds
historians greatly of Machiavelli's Italy.
Both eras in history were times of shifting
alliances, broken treaties, and unscrupulous

machinations. Among all the princes Frederick
William proved himself to be one of the most
adept at the kind of diplomatic and military
games everyone seemed to be playing. Of course,
he had to be. His scattered territories were
stretched clear across northern Germany, from
the Meuse River to the East Baltic. His was
therefore in a quite precarious position
internationally.

During the period 1660-1688, Frederick
William played the game of statecraft by several
times shifting into and out of alliances with
Holland, England, France, Denmark, Spain,
Austria, Sweden, and various German states.
In other words, at one time or another, he
allied himself with most of the greater and
lesser powers of Europe. If one dominant
thread can be seen in all of this, it is the
tendency to follow his Protestant sympathies
and enter alliances with Holland and England
to protect Germany's western territories from
Louis XIV of France.

Given this general tendency in his
policies, it is not surprising that Frederick
William turned against his sometimes patron
Louis XIV of France in 1674. The "Sun King" of
the French had invaded the Palatinate in
southwest Germany. The French soldiers had
acted quite cruelly during this invasion.
This fact, taken together with Frederick
William's natural sympathies for the Dutch,
caused him to enter the struggle on the side
of Holland. Quickly, he proceeded to Strasbourg
to attack the French. The diplomats of France
quickly retaliated by moving to distract the
forces of Brandenburg-Prussia and managed
to convince the Swedes that it was a propitious
time for them to attack Brandenburg; for the
Elector and his armies were out of the country.
It is typical of the political morality of
the time that the Swedes immediately considered
this overture, despite the fact that they
had only recently signed a nonaggression pact

with the Elector. Sweden decided, after quick consideration, to go along with the French proposal. They invaded Brandenburg and decimated the land, marauding armies inflicting barbarities on the local subjects.

It might be assumed that the various nobles and lords who were in the Electorate at the time this happened would have rallied to the general defense. They did not. Instead the nobility used this opportunity to seize what powers they could back from Frederick William, particularly in such matters as raising private feudal-type fighting forces on their own. To the great surprise and con-siderable consternation of the nobles, however, the peasants of Brandenburg rose up in defense of their ruler and his Electorate. They formed armed bands of their own. They devised their own "electoral" flags. Then the lowly tillers of Brandenburg's soil marched about singing a ditty: "We are only peasants and little land have we; but we give our blood for our lord right cheerfully."

Of course, Frederick had to gather his troops together and return as rapidly as possible from Brandenburg to meet these new threats. He finally caught the surprised Swedes on June 28, 1675, at a place called Fehrbellin. There he faced some 8,000 Swedish troops with 6,000 of his own. It was a dif-ficult battle for the Elector. He was now fifty-five years old, and often in pain from gout attacks. Yet he remained in the saddle for three weeks at the head of his men. And he rushed the more numerous Swedes at the head of his troops, waving his sword above his head and shouting: "Forward! Your prince and captain conquers with you--or dies like a knight!" The Elector did not die like a knight at Fehrbellin, however. Instead, he won a decisive victory. After this signal triumph he was known as "The Great Elector."

By 1677, he had swept the Swedes from
Pomerania.

Frederick William's final encounter
with the Swedes transpired in 1679. This
time his northern enemies struck not at
Brandenburg, but rather at Prussia. In the
winter of 1678-1679 Louis XIV had encouraged
the Swedes to ship an army of 16,000 across
the Baltic to invade Prussia from the north-
east. Frederick William covered some 400
miles in two weeks from Berlin to arrive in
time to save his eastern holdings. Fortu-
nately, luck was with him. The Swedish armies
were stalled outside the important Prussian
city of Köningsberg, having gorged themselves
with local pigs and thereby having become
infested with trichinosis. After having
marched his men 400 miles, Frederick William
led his forces an additional 100 miles across
snow and ice on 1,200 wooden sleds. The
Swedes were struck hard and sent back across
the Baltic out of Prussia. Unfortunately,
even though he had scored another decisive
victory, the Elector was forced soon thereafter to trade the domain of Western
Pomerania he had taken from Sweden for his
own territory of Cleves, which had been
occupied by Louis XIV while he was busy with
the Swedish armies. The Sun King demanded
that Frederick William's power be reduced
by ceding Western Pomerania back to Sweden.
The Elector did not wish to leave his subjects
in Cleves in the lurch; he unhappily did what
Louis had asked.

* * * * * * * *

Although the wars of the Great Elector
had not secured all the things for his country
that he might have wished, they did have the
effect of gaining the respect of the rest
of Europe for his own military powers and
the potential of his state for making war.

As we have seen, the title "Great Elector" was given to him because of his feats in battle, but it might have been given him for his enlightened internal policies as well.

Frederick William's enlightened administration was demonstrated by his liberalization of laws which benefited industry, agriculture, and trade. The way he used soldiers in peacetime also demonstrated the ingenuity he brought to statecraft. Members of his standing army were used to dig canals, the most important being the famous Frederick William Canal connecting the Elbe and Oder rivers. This remarkable feat, considering the limited technological achievements of the Elector's day, made Berlin into the center of water transportation between Central Europe and the old Hense port city of Hamburg. Frederick William's troops were also used to transform the Tiergarten area in Berlin into a pleasant park and provided a connection between it and central Berlin bordered by linden trees (the famous *Unter den Linden*").

The Elector's enlightened policies were also revealed in his acts of religious tolerance in an era when that sort of attitude was not very common among the rulers of Europe. He was a devout Protestant. Nevertheless, he permitted Catholics and Jews to live in his territories. Eventually, this liberal attitude led directly to a policy which greatly strengthened his Electorate.

In 1685, Louis XIV of France, whose later years were typified by an increasing religious intolerance, revoked the Edict of Nantes, a policy dictating religious toleration among the French which had been in effect for nearly a century. The rights of the Protestants in Louis' kingdom were thus withdrawn. The Calvinists of France, the Huguenots, were often imprisoned as a result and commonly were forced to become galley slaves, rowing

themselves to death on French ships. Thousands
of the Huguenots were sent searching for new
homes in this way. Frederick William quickly
condemned the French action and offered asylum
to any Huguenot who wished to come to his
domains. To help them accomplish this,
Frederick William aided these religious
refugees by sending them guides and travel
money. When they arrived in Berlin, numbering
some 20,000 in all, the Elector gave them
land, provided building materials, and freed
them from taxation for six years after their
coming. The Huguenots quickly became involved
in bettering the economic and cultural level
of the Electorate as many of them possessed
skills the state of Brandenburg-Prussia had
not known in abundance before.

* * * * * * * *

In sum, Frederick William was a violent
and often unjust ruler by modern standards.
But he was always concerned with the well-
being of his people. This characteristics
was certainly not a common one to be found
among the rulers of later-seventeenth century
European kingdoms. It was he who set the
Hohenzollerns on the path for greatness. It
was he who put the stamp of absolutism on
Brandenburg-Prussia, centralizing the administration and making the state militaristic
to maintain its power. From his reign forward,
the state never lost the seal of militarism
he had placed upon it. When he died in 1688,
he left behind him in the hands of his
successors a degree of militaristic-absolutistic
power which was never effectively tampered
with by the people of Prussia as was to be
the case in France during the revolutionary
era of 1789-1795.

The awareness of later Prussian monarchs
of the contribution of Frederick William is
seen in an incident transpiring some 100 years

later. The most important of all the
Hohenzollern monarchs, Frederick the Great,
in a sentimental moment, had the casket of
the Great Elector opened. He gazed at the
features of the Elector, still well preserved
after a century, and told those standing with
him, as he touched the dead hand of his
ancestor: "Gentlemen, this one performed
great works!" As was so often the case, the
comments of Frederick the Great were accurate
ones.

CHAPTER III

"KING IN PRUSSIA"

Conflict between the reigning sovereign
and the son who would inherit the throne,
as well as singular differences in personality,
were built into the situation existing in
late seventeenth-century royal houses.
Opponents of a ruling monarch, and others
who were simply discontented, rather naturally
gravitated toward his successor. Their hope
was to influence the heir to look more favorably
upon them and their causes than had his predecessor. Over a period of time, since the
son was often surrounded by "outs," people
the monarch distrusted, the king could be
influenced by the "ins" of his own circle
to see his offspring's accession to the throne
as a personal threat. It was not uncommon
for such rulers to believe that the monarch-to-be
would tear down the edifice of his own lifetime
of "good works." It was also not uncommon
for such rulers to believe that the monarch-to-be
looked upon the eventual and unavoidable demise
of his father with considerable pleasure.

The classic case of this kind of natural
conflict and distinct personality difference
between the ruler and his heir in all of
European history is to be discussed eventually
in these pages--the clash between Frederick
the Great and his father Frederick William I.
It was, however, a marked trait of the
Hohenzollern dynasty that, even given the
natural father-son conflict in monarchies,
the heir became something more than a contrast
there to the ruling prince than he tended
to be elsewhere in Europe. Sometimes this
worked out well for Prussia, the son providing
the qualities the father had lacked and that
the state needed. But that was not always
the case. It is true that Frederick III

(1688-1713) did provide for the state certain things that his father, the Great Elector, had not. On the whole, however, he was not nearly the talented ruler his parent had been.

* * * * * * * *

In the year 1657, when the Great Elector still had thirty-one years more to rule over Brandenburg-Prussia, a third child, Frederick, was born to the Electress Louise. Her first born had died in infancy and her second, Charles Emil, the heir apparent, was eventually killed in battle during the Great Elector's wars. Therefore it was not known at the time, but this Frederick who was born on July 11, 1657, would one day be the Elector.

The baby Frederick was about six months old when his parents took him from Berlin to the Baltic outpost of Königsberg, a journey of several hundred miles over terrible roads. In fact, roads of that era were so filled with deep holes that one could make better time by riding cross-country on a horse. These roads were popularly known at the time as "corduroy ways." They were so bad that the royal carriage constantly bounced around severely as it traversed on that fateful journey to Königsberg. Finally, after one particularly bad jolt, the nurse who held the infant prince lost control of him and the baby fell out of her arms, injuring his back so badly that he afterward grew to a misshapen manhood.

Because of the fact that he looked somewhat like a hunchback and was enormously frail as a child, Frederick was always pampered by his mother. Unfortunately, she died when he was only nine. His older brother, Charles Emil, who was kind and affectionate toward his younger and deformed sibling, died at age nineteen while fighting at Strasbourg.

By that time, the Great Elector had taken
a second wife, Dorthea of Holstein-Glücksburg.
When it became apparent that young Frederick
was the heir to the Electorate, Dorthea began
to intrigue against him.   It was her obvious
hope that one of her own sons by the Great
Elector could gain the domains of Brandenburg-
Prussia.   Naturally, given this state of affairs,
Frederick clashed with his stepmother.   In
time, gossip developed in court circles about
their quarrels.   It was said, probably with
some justification, that Dorthea would have
liked to have seen Frederick dead.   It is
possible that Dorthea, on at least one occasion,
attempted to poison the heir and that he
survived the attempt only because of the timely
use of an emetic.   Since Dorthea, and the
increasingly sterm Frederick William, opposed
the French in their policies, it was only
natural that the heir apparent should become
pro-French.

Frederick's pro-French attitudes soon
became obvious in his married life.   When
Sophia Charlotte of Hanover became his bride,
Dorthea slandered the young princess with
the rumor that she was not a virgin.   This
slander transpired at a time when the virginity
of the females in ruling circles was most
highly prized so that there would be no doubt
as to the "pure" royal blood of any offspring.
Frederick became so angered at such insults
that he withdrew from his father's court and
asked Louis XIV of France to become the godfather of his first child.   Perhaps Frederick
would not have been so pro-French had he known
that Louis had secretly bribed Dorthea to use
her influence at court with the Great Elector.
But the heir to the throne did not know of
this intrigue and thus remained stongly pro-
French, at least for the time being.   Eventually,
Frederick found out that Louis had rained
gifts on his despised stepmother.   That

discovery shifted him around to support of the Austrian emperor's cause.

* * * * * * * *

When Frederick inherited the Electorate in 1688, he became the third Elector to be called by that name. Elector Frederick III also received as a legacy from his father the improved financial and military machinery the former ruler had built. This situation gave Frederick III substantial income for the next nine years. It also provided him with such excellent credit that he could borrow large sums. This he did; for he quickly demonstrated a characteristic tendency for making very lavish expenditures.

Some of those people who are involved in the psychological analysis of historical figures have been very interested in Elector Frederick III. The general assessment among these psycho-historians seems to be that the career of the "deformed dandy," as he has been called, was one long-drawn-out attempt to hide his deformity under richness and glitter. Whether it was this tendency or an attempt, which would have been very common in this era, to imitate and/or outdo the antics and splendor of the Sun King, Louis XIV of France, Frederick III did attempt to reign over his state in the manner of the French monarch, gloriously. He thus teetered around the court in high-heel shoes as did Louis. He, like Louis, wore elaborate wigs, costly garments, and made every effort to upgrade his surroundings in Berlin to the Bourbon level, no matter what the cost. All of this took a great deal of time. He therefore turned over the running of Brandenburg-Prussia to Eberhard von Danckelman, a remarkable man who had considerable influence over the Elector during the first nine years of his reign.

As far as affairs of state were
concerned, Frederick had only one overriding
ambition; he wanted to be king. There were,
however, no kings in Germany. Only the Holy
Roman Emperor could make him a king. Fortu-
nately, for Frederick's ambitions, the Habsburg
emperor, Leopold I, was in dire need of allies
when Frederick came to power. The emperor
and William of Orange had decided to drive
Louis XIV out of Germany and the Netherlands.
Frederick was persuaded to place his troops
at the service of the emperor. He personally
led his forces into battle near Bonn against
the French and, by all accounts, acted with
bravery under fire.

The troops of the Elector remained
in the service of the Austrian emperor for
years. This proved to be a valuable addition
to the Habsburg forces, and Leopold appreciated
that fact. Eventually, Frederick used 8,000
of his men to bargain for the kingship.
Apparently, Frederick's yearning for the
kingship had been heightened by observing
his neighbors in ruling circles, some of whom
had just been elevated in station. For example,
the Duke of Brunswick had been elevated to
be Elector of Hanover in 1692. His son was
already the prospective George I of England.
Perhaps most important from Frederick's point
of view, the nearby Saxon elector had forsaken
Lutheranism in 1697 to become the King of
Poland. Frederick did have technical problems,
however, in his quest for the kingship. He
could not become the King of Brandenburg as
well as Prussia because Brandenburg was within
the territorial limits of the Holy Roman
Empire. The only king within that empire
was the Emperor himself who was also King
of Bohemia. All the other rulers owned
differing titles; they were variously electors,
dukes, princes, margraves, and others. Thus,
if Frederick wanted to become king, he had
to become king outside the original lands
of the Hohenzollerns. The most likely

possibility was Prussia, a territory actually
outside the Empire where Frederick was the
hereditary Duke. However, Prussia was not
the focal point of his rule. Brandenburg
was the center of his power. Moreover, he
ruled only in East Prussia, as West Prussia
was ruled by the Polish King. If Frederick
was to become the King of Prussia, he would
find himself in the somewhat ludicrous position
of being ruler of only half of his dominion
along the Baltic.

Considerations like these might have
convinced a ruler less set upon the kingship
to give up the ghost. Frederick would not
surrender his ambition, however, and he worried
constantly about how he might achieve it.
Finally, he decided that he would tell the
Emperor that he would become King in Prussia
rather than the King of it. At the same time,
he would remain the Elector of Brandenburg.
This half-fiction seemed to bother no one
very much and, for his part, Emperor Leopold I
appeared to regard the matter as a petty one.

Frederick was given his opportunity
to become a king by the death of Carlos II
of Spain in November of 1700. The Emperor
claimed the Spanish succession for Austria.
He wanted to use Frederick's 8,000 fighting
men to help secure his claim to the Spanish
throne. To get these men he agreed to recognize
the royal title when Frederick proclaimed
himself King in Prussia. Frederick lost little
time. On January 18, 1701, he set off for
Königsberg and his coronation. It is an odd
footnote to the whole business of Frederick's
becoming king that more horses were assembled
to mark his passing during the trip to the
crowning site (30,000) that the city of Berlin
had inhabitants. These aminals were positioned
all along the 400-mile route. Once in the
castle at Königsberg, as he saw a chance to
emphasize his independence of the church,
the king placed a crown upon his own head and

another upon his wife's. Nearly endless
formalities had been devised for the ceremony.
As the royal couple moved through them, the
new queen demonstrated her boredom with the
whole process by concentrating on dipping
into her snuff box. In this way the Elector
Frederick III became King Frederick I.

* * * * * * * *

        Was all of this a meaningless formality
designed to satisfy one man's inordinate vanity?
It would be a mistake to think that the
crowning was no more than that. It was an
age when such formalities counted for a great
deal. The coronation marked a real increase
in the power, the international prestige,
of the Brandenburg-Prussian state. Finally,
the Electorate had been given the rank in
Europe it had been entitled to since the days
of the Great Elector. Even some of Frederick's
contemporaries recognized what the new dignity
meant immediately. Struck with the importance
of what had happened, Prince Eugene of Savoy,
the Emperor's Field Marshal of greatest repute,
evaluated the coronation as follows: "the
imperial ministers who advised the Emperor
to recognize the King of Prussia should be
hanged!" Eugene of Savoy had been right about
the event's importance. Soon enough, though
only meant to be King in Prussia, Elector
Frederick II came to be known everywhere in
common usage as Frederick I, King of Prussia.
The administration in his provinces came to
be known as the "Royal Prussian Administration"
and the name Brandenburg was dropped as the
crown tied the scattered wings of Brandenburg-
Prussia more closely together in at least
the theoretical sense. As it turned out,
Frederick had brought with the royal crown
the common designation "Prussians" for the
people over whom he ruled. That Frederick
had schemed that so much would come out of
his becoming a king is dubious. In the short

term the thing that seemed to make him the
happiest was that he could now be addressed
as "Your Magesty," just as was Louis XIV.

Frederick also had secured from the
Holy Roman Emperor the privilege of having
a number of the lawsuits appearing in his courts
exempt from the usual appeals to the higher
imperial court. By 1703, Frederick had
replaced the appelate function of the Empire
with a new high court of his own. This
constituted a major step towards the centralization of justice and power. It indicates that
the deformed dandy had done more than simply
place a crown on his own head in 1701.

When the King returned from his coronation
at Königsberg, the residents of Berlin did
him great, if prearranged, honor. He rode
majestically through some six ornamental gates.
Thousands cheered wildly. The bells of the
churches rang out as some 200 cannon thundered
from the city walls. The elector had left
in December. A king had returned in May.

* * * * * * * *

Even before he had been crowned king,
Frederick had been busy making Berlin a place
fit to house a monarch. Of course, his father,
the Great Elector, had done much to improve
his capital. Frederick William had built
defensive fortifications around the city.
Moreover, as mentioned earlier, he had
accomplished much beautification by such devices
as the laying out of the Unter den Linden
avenue. In the palace he had established
a valuable public library which owned rare
oriental manuscripts.

Frederick I was ambitious to do much
more of this kind of thing than his father
had done. He spent large sums on public edifices
and palaces. He invited a well-known sculptor

44

and architect to the city, Andreas Schlüter, who built Sophia Charlotte a palace (called *Charlottenburg* today) in the baroque style for which the man was famous. From 1699 to 1705, when she died, the Charlottenburg palace became the center of the Queen's activities. There she surrounded herself with handsome men who often graced the royal bed. This would hardly be worth noting in an age which had the moral standards for monarchs set by the sexual antics in Louis XIV's magnificent court at Versailles, had it not been for the fact that the royal heir, the eventual King Frederick William I, stood by, with his strict Calvinist standards, condemning his mother's actions. Young Frederick William loathed all the exquisite laces and perfumes of Charlottenburg. He believed luxury was a direct symptom of corruption. He thought his father was a spendthrift and a fool. His mother he knew to be an adultress. Moreover, he hated the attempts of Frederick I and his wife to make their court into a cultural center.

Historians are not nearly so hard on this royal pair as was the future King of Prussia. Whatever her bedroom habits might have been, Sophie Charlotte had an unusual personal charm and she displayed an intense interest in literature and philosophy. In consequence, she attracted to the court many famous scholars, men of fashion, and artists. Gottfried Wilhelm von Leibnitz, the most noted German scholar of his day, was a friend of Sophie Charlotte's. Leibnitz was a versatile genius, noted for his accomplishments in theology, history, philosophy and statesmanship. Perhaps his crowning achievement was the discovery of calculus. In imitation of the French Academy at Paris Frederick established the Prussian Academy of Sciences and made Leibnitz its first president. Leibnitz remained in Berlin until his patroness, the Queen, died. After that, he moved to Hanover where he lived out the rest of his life.

Frederick I also founded the University of Halle in 1694. That act provided the ruler with a university in each of his principal provinces. Halle soon became distinguished, both for its liberal theology and progressive study of the law. It was in this university that, during the rule of Frederick I, lectures were given for the first time in German instead of Latin. At this point in time, this practice constituted a defiance of established tradition.

As soon as Andreas Schlüter had finished Sophie Charlotte's great salon Frederick gave him a new project. He was to build a copy of the Louvre. This building, the Zeughaus, was placed at the head of the Unter den Linden near the monarchical palace.

All of these activities enriched the state immeasurably in the cultural sense. They also, however, cost considerable sums of money. Frederick was obviously trying to equal the splendor of Versailles in his own kingdom, and he did so through more than simply building palaces. His buildings were furnished with extravagant furniture drawn from all over the world. He put together a massive collection of diamonds. He established a private zoo. Moreover, the massive outflow of money was enhanced by the actions of three ministers who were experts in piling up state debts. These advisors were named Wartenberg, Wartenslebe, and Wittgenstein. Since their names all began with the same letter, they were popularly known as the "three W's." In German this sounds a bit like the three woes, and such a title would have been most appropriate. These advisors were certainly that. They managed to double the household expenditures and fill their own pockets at the same time. They were finally exposed and thrown out in 1711 as a result of an investigation conducted by the frugal and horrified crown prince himself.

* * * * * * * *

The considerable expense incurred by
Frederick I was paid for in part by subsidies
granted him by foreign powers so that they
could make use of the Prussian army in their
international adventures. A dependence on
subsidies from foreign patrons meant that
the King had very little freedom of action.
This fact was demonstrated in 1700 when the
Second Northern War broke out. It was further
demonstrated a year later when the War of
the Spanish Succession began.

In the Second Northern War the ambitious
Charles XII of Sweden had attacked and defeated
the Russians under Peter the Great at Narva.
The Swedish King then proceeded to conquer
Poland and set up camp on the Prussian border
in Saxony. At about the same time, in the
west, Carlos II had died and rival claims
to the Spanish throne arose, the claimants
being the French, Habsburgs, and Bavarians.
The Dutch and English also took up an important
role in this conflict as Louis XIV thoughtlessly
recognized the Stuart pretender as King of
England upon the death of William of Orange
in 1702.

Frederick I's true interests lay in
the conflict between Sweden and Russia. If
he took the Russian side, he might have gained
valuable territories to add to his holdings
in the east. But since he was so tied to
subsidies and the Russians were unwilling
to pay him, he was forced to enter the War
of the Spanish Succession in the west where
the Austrian ruler was willing to meet his
price. The western choice was not without
at least some merit. By it, the Prussian
King could continue the Great Elector's policy
of defending Protestantism and Germany. Moreover, through this policy he could press his
claims to certain of the lands belonging to

the Orange family. Hence, the Prussians
entered the struggle for the Spanish throne
and fought with distinction all over Europe.
At the Peace of Utrecht in 1713 Prussia did
obtain small portions of the Orange lands,
tiny parcels here and there in an area
stretching from Switzerland to the Netherlands.

In the Northern War Charles XII was
eventually pulled deep into southern Russia.
There he was defeated at Poltava in 1709.
Thereafter, he fled to Turkey where he lived
in exile for five years. As all of this was
going on, Russians and Poles were invading
Swedish Pomerania. In the short term, Prussia
could do nothing about this violation of the
Empire's neutrality in the Second Northern
War, because its troops were committed in
the west. Thus was underlined Prussia's over-
dependence on subsidies and her inability
to act even in her own backyard. Ultimately,
Prussia was drawn into the last stages of
the Russo-Swedish War, but this was only after
the death of Frederick I and during the reign
of his son.

* * * * * * * *

The last years of King Frederick I
were unhappy ones. His treasury was depleted
by his spendthrift regime. Many of his people
were resentful of his glittering life style.
The contrast, and possible relationship, between
the increased splendor of Berlin and the reduction in the general prosperity was not lost
on many observers. In fact, what general
prosperity there still was, and Prussia yet
compared fairly favorably with other German
states, derived primarily from the reign of
the Great Elector. The King did take some
pleasure from being a grandfather. He lived
long enough to see his grandson, the boy who
would one day be Frederick the Great, born
to Frederick William and Sophia Dorthea of

Hanover. In fact, he was so overjoyed at
the birth of a proper heir that he had little
"Fritz's" umbilical cord put into a silver
vessel bearing upon it the date and time of
the baby's birth.

Before his grandson was born, however,
Frederick I had taken another wife for himself
to provide an heir for the house of Hohenzollern if his son and his wife could not
manage to do so. When he married for the
second time, he was fifty-one years old, sickly,
weak, and, of course, deformed. He new wife
was twenty-four-year-old Sophia Louise of
Mecklenburg-Schwerin. Unfortunately, the
King's new bride turned out to be quite mad.
When it became apparent that his new wife
was mentally unstable, and it became apparent
all too soon that this was the case, the King
saw to it that she spent most of her time
far away from him, secluded in her apartments.
Finally, one morning, his deranged wife escaped
from the attendants delegated to guard her.
She ran through the palace corridors toward
the King's bedroom where she crashed through
a glass door leading to his chamber. In the
process of doing that she cut herself quite
badly. Blood began running down over her
white nightgown. The King awoke, startled,
to see what appeared to be an apparition before
him. He shouted something about the "White
Lady," apparently thinking his young wife
to be the resident ancestral ghost of the
Hohenzollerns who supposedly appeared before
each of them to announce their approaching
deaths. The King fell senseless, the victim
of an attack. A few days later he was dead
and his son, Frederick William I, had come
to the throne of Brandenburg-Prussua. Thus
died a monarch who was neither the best of
kings or the worst. Perhaps as good as judgment
on him as any was the one made by his grandson,
Frederick the Great: "He was little in great
things, great in little things."

CHAPTER IV

THE "GARRISON KING"

Frederick William I was born on August 14, 1688. He was the only son of Frederick I and his wife Sophie Charlotte. By the time that he had succeeded to the throne in 1713, he had come to hate with a passion the man the German historians often have called "Frederick the Ostentatious" because of that monarch's taste for pomp and grandeur. Frederick William was not willing to excuse such tastes or try to understand them in the way Frederick the Great did later on when he wrote of his grandfather that: "He imagined that by choosing this monarch [Louis XIV] for his model he could not fail to be praised in like manner." But this Frederick I who aimed at being the "Grand Monarch" of Germany by surrounding himself with numerous courtiers, chamberlains, grooms of the chamber, pages, and countless other fawning people only served by his actions to disquiet and anger his son.

From his earliest days Frederick William was surrounded by wealth and privilege, by flatterers and fawners. His every primitive and obsessive emotion was indulged. For example, at the age of four, when his governess was dressing him, he refused to be dissuaded from sticking the silver buckle of one of his shoes in his mouth. When his nanny tried to take it from him, he swallowed it. Not surprisingly, there was great anxiety at the court for a few days. Somehow, however, he managed to rid himself of the buickle without doing any discernible damage. Similarly, in another instance, he was deprived of his breakfast for having committed some sort of misdemeanor. His answer to that punishment was to climb

51

out on a window ledge some three stories up and threaten to jump unless he was fed immediately. Rather than lose an heir, his governess gave in.

Neither the young prince's parents or his tutors were much more successful than his nanny in taming the spirit of this spoiled brat. On one occasion he was provided with the Prince of Kurland for a playmate. He immediatly began administering a severe beating to the young prince. When his mother saw this happening, she asked him mildly: "My dear son, what are you doing?" Untroubled, the heir finished the thrashing of the young prince. A bit later he pushed a court official down a flight of stairs, severely injuring that gentleman's neck. His mother only scolded him gently.

Frederick William was provided with the best of tutors. He was brought up for the most part by a French nurse, a French tutor, and a Prussian noble who was primarily responsible for him (Count Alexander von Dohna). He quickly demonstrated for these people his great resistance to learning. They made him study French. But, once he had learned it, he Germanized the language when he wrote it. He established a well-deserved reputation for terrible grammar and spelling. When his tutors objected to these tendencies, he would fly into a rage and denounce them. Or he would threaten them. One of his favorite threats was: "May the devil take me if I do not have all of you hanged or your heaads cut off when I grow up." He also liked to threaten that he would take poison or strangle himself in such a way that his tutors would be blamed for his death. He was a husky lad and from time to time he would become violent with his tutors. When he did this, he would kick them, tear off their wigs, butt them with his royal head, hit them with his fists, beat them with anything at hand, or even try to strangle them. His temper was so instantaneously aroused that, if he could not lay his hands on a tutor when angered, he would simply begin ramming his head into a wall. How the royal brains remained unscrambled during all of this has never been adequately explained. Indeed, he was a thorough little monster. But it is one of the paradoxes of history that this terrible brat turned out to be a very good king.

It is true that, by the time he became king, he was overly accustomed to having his own way. He had little self-control. He did nothing moderately. One ambassador wrote home about the Prussian ruler that: "Whatever he desires, he desires vehemently." He expected instant and blind obedience and the slightest opposition drove him to a frenzy. When so convulsed, he would use a stout cane he carried with him always to shower blows on those who had committed blunders or otherwise aroused his ire. The Austrian ambassador, seeing this, was moved to write home: "At times, this king must be out of his mind." When anything was said to the King about his tendencies toward irrational behavior, and only a court chaplain or some other man of the cloth would dare scold him, he would say that his behavior was simply the result of the inborn sinfulness of man. He would reply: "You are right, but that is simply my nature."

Unlike his grandfather, Elector Frederick William, or his son, King Frederick II, no one ever decided to call this man "The Great." Nonetheless, this irascible, seemingly half-mad tyrant was the author of many great accomplishments and without his works Frederick II, his son, could never have elevated Prussia to great-power status in Europe.

* * * * * * *

At this juncture it should prove useful to evaluate the progress of the House of Hohenzollern as the reign of the "Garrison King" of Prussia began in 1713. The history of the family had begun with an ancestral home in a Swabian castle near the sources of the Danube and the Neckar. Eventually, the Hohenzollerns had become electors of the Holy Roman Empire, which is in itself something of an accomplishment. For a long time, however, their electorate was backward, poor, and not especially well regarded by most of the monarchs who counted in Europe. Recently, however, the Prussians, with the reign of the ambitious little Frederick I, had become kings. That fact still, however, did not mean very much internationally. Nevertheless, the modern Prussian state was about to appear at this point and to be built by this strange man whose nature was so violent, whose cane crashed down unmercifully and indiscriminately on the backs of his subjects. And this Prussia was to be the nucleus around which was built the modern German Reich of the Kaisers.

The King who was to do so much to build Prussia into a powerful state was a strict Calvinist, whose reverence for God's power did not in any way interfere with his puritanic temper. As a strict Calvinist he early developed a loathing for all finery and for the loose life of his father's court. When his father and mother and those around them were doing their best to look like Lous XIV, Frederick William was greasing his face with bacon fat and sitting in the sun so that he might be tanned like a soldier. He so hated finery that, as a boy, when ordered to put on a gold brocade dressing gown one morning, he demonstrated his displeasure at the idea by tossing the garment into the fire. Frederick William also disliked the shams, cabals, deceits, and intrigues of his father's court and he tried to free his own reign from these traits.

This new king believed in very hard work. He labored mightily and he expected everyone in his administration to do likewise. As his first order of business, he gave his father a very find funeral, the kind of send-off the deformed dandy would likely have admired very much. No sooner was his father buried than the new king hurried to the palace to begin work. He announced that he had no time for a coronation. Uppermost in his mind seemed to be the idea of saving what such a festival would have cost. Once in the palace he personally helped the servants to take down various ornate draperies and wall hangings. He quickly put the former King's diamonds, wines, and other valuable items on the market, peddling many of his father's baubles to Augustus the Strong of Saxony. For good measure, since Frederick William apparently believed he would not need them, he sent along one of his father's men, an old master of ceremonies who had arranged protocol and etiquette for the former ruler. His first official letter informed the Prince of Anhalt that Frederick William intended to become his own Minister of Finance as well as "Commander in Chief [of the army] to the King of Prussia." The new King very quickly had a hand in everything else, including the church, education, and justice. From the time he was eight years of age he had kept a personal record entitled "Account of my Ducats." The attitude that had produced this ledger now transformed the state.

For a quarter of a century, from 1688 to 1713, the young heir had grown up surrounded by continual plans for making war or going to war. During that time, he had become more than a little distressed with the fact that Prussia's army, indeed her entire foreign policy, was dependent on foreign subsidies. In keeping with his generally thrifty nature, Frederick William I wanted to make Prussia independent of the subsidies upon which she had depended so heavily during the days of his father. He wanted Prussia to possess a war treasury of its own and, at the same time, own an army sufficiently large and powerful to protect his state. Only with a powerful army, the new King reasoned, would Prussia follow her own interests. Practially, this policy worked out to be a peaceful one. Frederick William was involved in the last stages of the Northern War. After that, he remained at peace. When he came to the throne in 1713, he inherited a bankrupt administration. The army stood at 40,000 men. Upon his death in 1740, his son, Frederick the Great, inherited a model administration and an army numbering 83,000, a fighting force generally regarded as the most efficient and best in all of Europe.

His first step in improving the army was to place Prince Leopold of Anhalt-Dessau (the "Old Dessauer" as he was called) over it. The Old Dessauer was a famous veteran of many battles. From 1693, when he was only seventeen years old, Leopold had served as a battlefield commander and as a military innovator. Leopold fought on until he was seventy, the age at which he entered his last battle under Prussian colors. The superb Prussian army which Frederick the Great was to use so effectively owed its existence more to Anhalt-Dessau than any other man. The old Dessauer seemed to some almost a mirror image of Frederick William himself. He was also bluff, unrefined, and direct. And he had been Frederick William's friend for some years before the King came to power. Anhalt-Dessau was quickly put in charge of the army as soon as Frederick William came to the throne. He immediately installed a program of intense drilling and training. "Fire well, reload qui:kly" soon became fmailiar words, drummed into the head of every Prussian soldier. It was Dessauer who reintroduced marching in cadence, something that the Roman legions had done. After the Romans, however, the practice had fallen into disuse over the centuries. Making columns march in step allowed them to be wheeled around and maneuvered effectively with potentially devastating effects on the opposition.

The King and Anhalt-Dessau had similar views on discipline. Both believed in using physical force to produce obedience. The Old Dessauer used beatings to turn his recruits into superbly drilled automatons. The King used canings similarly on those around him who did not work as strenuously as he did.

* * * * * * * *

Frederick William had already been hard to work for two years and more before he became monarch to rid the Prussian kingdom of the worst administrative abuses devised by the three woes. A consolidation of the civil revenue administration was begun at that time and completed as soon as he was king in fact. He also went to work reorganizing his own private holdings, making sure that they had strict and honest supervision, so that returns from the royal lands were doubled in just two years.

It is typical of Frederick that, as soon as he had acceded to the throne, he asked for a roll of the royal household to be brought before him. It was a long list and he drew his pen through two-thirds of the names. Many of those dismissed were at once placed in the army. When he apprised the courtiers of his decisions, he told them forcefully: "The new king sends every one of you to the devil!" Thereafter, the atmosphere in the Hohenzollern palace was so military that the handful of pages waiting on tables were assisted by some of the royal huntsmen and a number of grenadiers.

This reduction in the expenses at court
was simply a necessity and not merely a case
of kingly miserliness. Brandenburg-Prussia
had been left deeply in debt by Frederick I's
spendthrift ways. The son of the profligate
father saw clearly that Prussia could not
be the great cultural center his father had
wanted it to be and a strong military state
at the same time. He had therefore opted
for the powerful military and everything else
that did not support that end had to go.

The King's basic premise was that his
ends could not be achieved, he could not make
Prussia prosperous and pay off his father's
obligations, unless everyone in the kingdom
was utilized to the greatest extent possible.
To make certain that this full utilization
transpired, Frederick William looked into
almost every situation he could find that
might help create what he called a "plus"
for the state. A plus might be a market women
who, when not selling her wares in the market-
place, was ordered personally by the King
to keep busy knitting socks. So that people
might be kept devising ways to use their time
more profitably for Prussia, pastors were
ordered to preach for no more than one hour
at a time. Those who became long-winded were
fined.

All servants of the crown, as was the
case with all his subjects, were inspired
with a deep fear of the King's authority and
his sense of duty, discipline, and punctuality.
He took walks through his capital regularly.
If he saw a man loafing, he seized him and
caned him personally. If he heard someone
who appeared to be wasting time quarreling
with his wife in his own home, he might well
throw open the doors to the house, run in,
and beat the quarrelers. On one occasion
the Saxon minister at Berlin reported the
following incident:

Everyday His Majesty gives
new proofs of his justice. Walking
recently at Potsdam at six in
the morning, he saw a post-
coach arrive with several passengers
who knocked for a long time
at the post-house which was
still closed. The King, seeing
that no one opened the door, joined
them in knocking and even knocked
in some window-panes. The master of
the post then opened the door and
scolded the travelers, for no one
recognized the King. But His
Majesty let himself be known by
giving the official some good blows
of his cane and drove him from his
house and his employment after
apologizing to the travelers for his
laziness. Examples of this sort, of
which I could relate several others,
makes everybody alert and exact.

Naturally, some of the people of Prussia
came to the point where they barred the windows
against the King, shut themselves up in their
houses, while a monarch like this was known
to be roaming the streets. His subjects
were simply frightened to death of him. Perhaps
perversely, Frederick William refused to
believe those in his service who reported
that his people feared him. He would brook
no suggestion that they did not love him.
There were, however, a mounting number of
incidents which proved that he was indeed
more feared than loved. Once while out walking
the King saw a man fleeing at his approach.
The poor wretch stumbled and fell. Frederick
William grabbed the fellow before he could
get away. The King asked him why he had
fled:

"I was afraid," came the reply.
"Afraid? Afraid?" the Monarch
  screamed.
"You are supposed to love me!"
"Love me, you scum?" he cried.

At that point, to secure the man's affection,
the ruler of Brandenburg-Prussia beat him
over the back with his cain.

Even Frederick William's closest and
most trusted advisors were frightened of
the King's possible wrath. Frederick William
always kept two pistols loaded with salt
by his side in his chambers. He is supposed
to have fired them off at any valet who did
not move quickly enough, one of them losing
an eye because of this particularly eccentric
habit. He was even known to cane the officers
of his army in full view of their own men.
One of these beaten soldiers was so shamed
by an incident like this that, after a kingly
thrashing, he drew two pistols. This unsettled
major then fired one pistol into the ground
in front of Frederick William and used the
other to blow a hole in his head.

All of this smacks of lunacy. But
behind the smokescreen of eccentricities
and near madness there moved a very efficient
ruler. Perhaps the most important characteristic of his personality is that he watched
over everything personally. His movements
were always canalized in the direction of
making his regime one which would preside
over prosperity and reside without fear behind
military strength. To accomplish those ends
military revenues were increased. In East
Prussia a new general land tax brought in
a vastly increased amount of money. Moreover,
the base of the new tax was a broader one.
Taxes became fairly uniform throughout the
kingdom. With more enlightened economic
policies, the people of the kingdom generally

became more prosperous. Increased prosperity
raised even more tax money. Mercantilist
measures were initiated to protect and foster
Prussia's own manufacturers at a time when
the boundaries of the state were too irregular
to permit a workable tariff policy. The
old medieval notion of the feudal levy, that
a knight owed his lord military service
sporadically, was abandoned in practice so
that the nobility could help the Prussian
state by paying a direct subsidy for the
army instead. Moreover, it became common
during the rule of Frederick William that
the nobles should serve the state as officers
in the army.

Early in his reign, Frederick William
consolidated all military, financial, and
administrative activities into a so-called
"General Directory." The General Directory
eventually became the most powerful instrument
the King used to govern. The Directory was
made up of four departments which were partly
regional and reflected the irregular territorial growth of Brandenburg-Prussia. Each
department had no existence of its own; it
simply prepared the business assigned to
it for a consideration of the Directory as
a whole. The establishment of this Directory
represented a real modernization of government
in the first half of the eighteenth century.

The Directory was not a real cabinet
in the modern sense, however. None of the
representatives of the four departments dared
contradict the King during their deliberations
with him. The closest thing in the Prussian
kingdom to a real cabinet was Frederick
William's so-called Tobacco Parliament.

The Tobacco Parliament met nightly
at Berlin, Potsdam, or Wusterhausen, wherever
the King was at a given moment. This body
was usually composed of the monarch's closest
advisors, mostly generals. When the weather

was sufficiently favorable, the Parliament
met outside. Otherwise the body was convened
in a large unadorned room. It became customary
for each guest to have set before him a large
pitcher of beer and a clay pipe. Baskets
of tobacco were placed on the table. Everyone
was expected to drink considerable quantities
to please the King and even to pull at an
empty pipe if the individual involved did
not smoke (as in the case of the Old Dessauer).
Frederick William, who would as soon smoke
his pipe as eat, often consumed as many as
thirty pipefuls of tobacco in one session.
The meetings served several purposes. They
were educational, a lecturer reading aloud
from foreign or German newspapers and journals.
They were typified by comradery, the hunt
or military life being favorite topics of
conversation. There was also much coarse
humor, the humor of the soldier and the hunter.
These gatherings gave the King so much pleasure
that, should he have become ill, he had himself carried to the meetings. And if he
was too sick even to attend his Parliament
on a stretcher, he had the members of his
group called to his sickroom.

A darker side of the activities in
the Tobacco Parliament was to be found in
the King's ill treatment of Jakob Paul
Gundling. Frederick William hated the Berlin
Academy of Science, which his father had
founded and had made famous by the importation
of the great scholar Leibnitz to direct it.
The Garrison King only continued the existence
of the Academy because an army surgeon had
convinced him that it would prove useful
in the training of military doctors. The
fact that the Prussian ruler continued the
despised Academy, however, did not keep him
from ridiculing it at every opportunity.
Whenever he could he demonstrated his contempt
for the body by such acts as entering the
salary of its members in the royal accounts
under the heading: "Expenses for the Royal
Buffoons." The choice of Gundling, a

dull-witted man, to be his head of the Academy
was yet another way of insulting the whole
idea of a learned body. Gundling, once
appointed, provided another way of achieving
the same end. He quickly became the target
of many coarse practical jokes perpetrated
by the King and his chums. This was only
fitting as far as the King was concerned.
To Frederick William, Gundling was one of
those men of learning the monarch categorized
as *Schwarzscheisser* ("men who defecate black").

   In the Tobacoo Parliament Gundling
was bombarded with indignities. One day
he would be elevated to the rank of Master
of Ceremonies at court and be dressed in
an elaborate and ridiculous uniform complete
with goats' hair, ostrich feathers, and high
heels. When publicly invested with his duties
while dressed in this fashion, he was presented
with an ape dressed in identical fashion.
The ape sat next to him at the table that
evening. Gundling's perseverance in all
this was eased by the soothing balm of imbibed
spirits. He had a taste for the fermented
grape and he was urged to get dead drunk
by the cronies of the Parliament nearly every
night. Once that goal was achieved, and
it nearly always was, the pranks would begin.
One night, for example, he was thrown into
bed completely inebriated. Two bear cubs,
their forepaws mutilated so that they could
not lacerate poor Gundling, were tossed into
bed with him and chained there. When he
awoke, he found in the bleary haze of a morning
after that he was sharing his bed with the
two cubs and they had fouled his sheets
considerably.

   Even when poor Gundling died in 1731,
apparently as the result of having ruined
his stomach with alcohol (a post-mortem ordered
by the King demonstrated a highly ulcerated
stomach), the funeral was made over into
another occasion of amusement for the membership

of the Tobacco Parliament. The King ordered
the corpse dressed in bright red satin upon
which was embroidered the letters WURM (worm).
The corpse was fitted with a red silk stocking-
cap and given a prodigious wig of goat's
hair. Then the body was placed in a sitting
position in a coffin shaped like a wine
cask. On the side of the cask was inscribed:

> In his own skin here lies
> Half swine, half man, a wonder-
> thing
> Wise in youth, foolish in old age
> Mornings full of wit, at night
> full of wine and rage.
> "Hark!" Bacchus loudly cries;
> "This precious child is Gundling."

Under Frederick William I, therefore, the
Tobacco Parliament became an odd combination
of coarse tricks and jests combined with
discussions that might well influence matters
of state. In this situation the General
Directory became less and less the source
of royal authority, since Frederick William
hardly ever bothered to attend its meetings.
One of the reasons for this was that the
Directory met in Berlin while Frederick William
was usually at Potsdam or one of his hunting
lodges. Under Frederick William, the tendency
became for the monarch increasingly to decide
matters himself. This would happen after
solitary deliberations in his own apartments
or after discussions in the Tobacoo Parliament.
What was happening was the extreme centralization
and increased absolutism oof the state. In
this kind of tendency is to be seen one of
the great flaws of absolutist government;
it tended to work fairly well under the constant
and alert supervision of intelligent and
hard-working monarchs like Frederick William I
and Frederick the Great. But so much depended
on one person and the government so closely
reflected the character of the King that,

under lesser rulers such as were the immediate
successors of the two Hohenzollerns who dominated
the eighteenth century, the tendency to center
the functions of the state so much in one
man proved unfortunate. In fact, the tendency
proved to be disastrous for Prussian fortunes
during the French Revolutionary and Napoleonic
periods.

* * * * * * * *

Of all the institutions he made operate
more effectively, the most important that
Frederick William shaped was the army. Frederick
William I has often been called, as has been
the case in these pages, the "Garrison King,"
or the "Royal Drill Sergeant." He was deserving
of those titles in that he gave to the army
a new spirit, discipline, and efficiency.
He began the accomplishment of his task with
the army early in his reign by purging the
officer corps of ineffective leaders. Many
of these men were foreign adventurers. In
their places he installed his own nobles
who were forbidden under pain of severe
penalities to hire themselves out as soldiers
to other rulers as was the common practice
in Frederick William's day. To make certain
that his noble officer corps would become
more or less an hereditary system, the Royal
Drill Sergeant installed a cadet corps in
Berlin. The military employment of his own
nobles helped to consolidate the bond between
the Prussian nobility and the army. It also
tended to eradicate the remnants of the old
feudal opposition of the rural lords to
centralized control from Berlin. Out of
this developed a Prussian (Junker) nobility
which, long accustomed to commanding the
peasants on their own estates, naturally
eased into the role of commanding the army.
Quickly enough, the officers' ranks in the
army became a Junker caste system, typified
by a sense of social superiority. Thereafter,

65

it was a symbol of the highest social prestige to be in the ranks of the Prussian army.

When Frederick William began to build up his army, recruiting was done by individual officers who often came into conflict with each other over potential recruits. To remedy such abuses Frederick William adopted in 1733 the Prussian Cantonal system. By it, the nation was divided into districts and each district had to supply the men for a particular regiment.

Prussian soldiers were taken mainly from among the peasants. They served in what was becoming one of the few large standing armies in Europe. There was, of course, a potential economic loss to the state to be chanced in withdrawing these men from agriculture. This loss was made less apparent by a provision worked out by Frederick William and his advisors so that the soldiers who had been completely trained were released on furlough for nine months each year. This situation allowed them to go home and till the land.

Frederick William built barracks in Berlin and quartered some soldiers in fortresses. By and large, however, soldiers were placed with families in various garrison towns. These quartered soldiers constituted no great burden for local families, however. They either paid for the food they ate or bought and prepared their own. Most towns were glad to welcome a regiment; for the soldier's spending greatly stimulated local economic life. This practice also had the effect of drawing the whole state into the support of the armed forces.

The army proved to be a world unto itself. Soldiers had their own laws, their own police, and their own justice. If a soldier erred he could be subject only to the laws of his army or, as supreme commander, the King's judgment. The King, however, was usually very quick to forgive when one of his soldiers was involved. In one typical case a musketeer known well for his abilities as a fighter had stolen 6,000 talers. The soldier-thief was sentenced to the usual penalty for such a crime; he was to be hanged. The man's colonel, loathe to lose such a battler, appealed the decision to Frederick William. The King summoned the judge who had sentenced his musketeer to court and berated him for being so harsh with a good soldier. In the process of his dressing-down of the magistrate he knocked out a few of the judge's teeth with his ever-ready weighted cane.

Given his love for the military, it is not particularly surprising that the King developed an unusual hobby; he collected extraordinarily tall soldiers for what came to be called the "Potsdam Giant Guards." He called recruits for his special unit his *lange Kerle*, his "long fellows." Well over six feet in height, they wore a tall pointed headgear above their powdered heads. In addition to a dagger and flint-lock musket they also carried a bag of hand grenades and, hence, were known as grenadiers. These giant soldiers were collected from Prussia itself, were actually purchased in other lands, were received as gifts from foreign rulers, or kidnapped almost anywhere in Europe and dropped off in Berlin. In fact, as many as 1,000 kidnappers worked for King Frederick William I at any one time with orders to abduct any man they could find who was over six feet tall. Few tall men who traveled Prussia during the reign of Frederick William were safe. In some instances, even foreign diplomats were abducted and impressed into the Giants Guard. If protests were made by their respective governments, then the King would suddenly release them, grumbling as he did so. Frederick William even went so far in

one instance as to have a tall monk spirited
out of a monastery in Rome.

It should come as no surprise to the
reader that many of these impressed tall men
were quite unhappy. One chaplain to the Roman
Catholics among the Guards, a Dominican named
Bruns, wrote in his diary about the incredible
despair felt by some of the unhappy men forced
into the Prussian ruler's pet unit. The
soldiers, wrote Bruns, were always trying
to burn the city of Potsdam down and/or kill
the King. By such rash actions, they hoped
against hope to gain their freedom and return
to their homelands. In fact, escapes sometimes
happened. Most who ran away were caught,
however. About 250 men attempted to escape
each year. If they were caught, their punishment was horrible; their noses and ears were
removed and they spent the rest of their lives
in Spandau prison. There were those in the
Giant Guards who could neither face the hazards
of escape or life in the regiment. Many of
these men simply took the first opportunity
to commit suicide. Frederick William was
always astounded that any of his soldiers
were "so evil" as to commit such rash acts
instead of accepting the honor of his service.

The Giant Guards were drilled mercilessly.
The King loved to do that job personally.
His eye was so sharp that he could spot any
imperfection in the drilling, any man slightly
out of line. He wanted at a command, as he
put it, to hear "only one click" along the
line and "only one report in platoon firing."
These techniques of drill after drill, beatings,
and terror tactics to enforce discipline,
worked out initially with the Giants, were
eventually extended to the rest of the army.
It became by far the best army in Europe
because of such tactics, although not very
many people knew that it was an excellent
fighting force because it was never tested
on the field of battle.

Other improvements also made the Prussian army an impressive military machine. Wooden ramrods for muskets, likely to break or catch fire, were replaced by iron ones. The bayonets, formerly fastened on the muzzle of the gun where they had to be removed before firing, were now fastened outside the barrel. This change allowed Prussian soldiers to advance closely when meeting the enemy, at the same time continuing their fire and then switching instantly to the use of steel without halting to fix bayonets. There were better cannon, better uniforms, and better techniques of battle such as the famed "Prussian Oblique," which allowed a smaller force to attack and easily defeat a larger one.

The Prussian army thus built actually frightened no ruler or general in Europe. Foreign powers saw Frederick William as too timid in international affairs ever to use it. But foreign powers were mistaken in dismissing this army so casually. It was this same fighting force that Frederick the Great would use one day to turn Europe upside-down.

* * * * * * * *

Frederick William was suspicious of everyone. Because of this fact he kept the reins of government firmly in his hands for his whole tenure as ruler. No one minded very much. The bourgeoisie had grown rich in commerce and industry. The Junkers had been drawn together as a group and any feudal residue of antagonism on their part for the monarchy seemed to have evaporated. The relationship between the Junkers and their King was a symbiotic one. The Junkers dominated the land and the King let them as long as they did not interfere with his absolute power over the army, followed his

69

royal regulations (he composed a book of
thirty-five chapters of them for the nobles),
and remained uninvolved in the affairs of
the towns. Therefore, everything purred along
efficiently in Prussia, the land of the
Garrison King. And government officials seemed
to be everywhere to make sure that this would
continue to be the case.

Frederick William's instructions were
precise and he wanted them followed precisely.
His officers were "responsible" for acting
out to the letter the orders he issued. What
would happen to officials who were in error
was indicated by a little drawing he had
doodled beside the word "responsible" in his
personal collection of regulations. The drawing
was of a gallows. Moreover, he took much
the same attitude with his Junkers. If they
did not do as he told them he planned: "to
make them dance to my tune or may the Devil
take them; if they do not, I shall treat them
as rebels, I shall hang them and roast them
as would the Tsar!" Apparently Frederick
William thought that none of these promised
actions was extreme because he was often heard
to complain that, as an administrator: "God
knows I am far too tranquil!" This meant
that he looked upon himself as too gentle
and forgiving to be an effective ruler.

In this fashion Prussia prospered and
Frederick William aged rapidly. The nights
spent swilling beer in the Tobacco Parliament
finally began to take their effect. He grew
wider year by year. At his death he weighed
273 lbs. and his waist measured some
102 inches. Moreover, he was far too short
to carry so much poundage. He thus looked
rather like a ponderous, bloated mass of flesh
out of which, seemingly, had popped a large
head. He had once had a robust constitution
which he had ruined through immoderate eating,
drinking, and smoking. He hence had become
prematurely aged and the fact was evident

to almost everyone, although hardly anyone
ever spoke of it. He suffered much from the
gout. In 1734, symptoms of dropsy set in.
Soon his legs had swelled, as he put it himself, to the size of "butter-tubs." The last
five years of his life he was constantly in
ill health.

During the early months of 1740,
Frederick William's illness grew much worse.
Finally, the King had to face the fact that
he was dying, an old man while only in his
early fifties. With typical Prussian
efficiency he set about making ready for the
end. These are the instructions he gave:

"1. As soon as I am dead, my body
is to be washed, dressed in a clean
shirt, and placed upon a wooden table;
then I am to be shaved and made
generally neat. That finished, I am
to be covered with a sheet and
permitted to remain that way from two
to four hours.

"2. In the presence of
Lieutenant-General von Bodenbruck,
Colonel von Derschau, Major von Bredow,
Captains von Prinzen and von Hacke, and
Lieutenant von Winterfeld, as well as
the physicians who are here and also
the surgeons of my regiment and my servants,
all of whom must be present, my body is
to be opened and carefully examined in
order to ascertain the real cause of my
death and the internal condition of my
body. But I forbid most emphatically
that any organ be taken out; only the
water and the phlegm, insofar as possible,
is to be removed; then my body is to be
washed, dressed in the best uniform I
possess, and put in the coffin, which is
not to be draped. This done, the lid of
the coffin is to be fastened with screws
and left that way throughout the night."

Frederick William continued in this
manner for pages, detailing every last aspect
of his funeral. Characteristically, he had
already set a precise sum of money aside for
his burial and the ceremonies surrounding
it.

By the time Frederick William I sensed
the approach of the grim reaper, all details
had been seen to personally. He relaxed and
soon slipped off into a coma. From time to
time he came out of it and asked the attending
doctors for a mirror so that he could view
himself and see if he looked any more like
a corpse than the last time he had looked.
He also demanded, in these moments of awareness,
reports on just how much he had slipped since
the last time he had asked. He cautioned
the physicians to be quite exact. Then he
was dead.

As was usually the case with a Prussian
ruler, there was much martial ceremony
surrounding the burial. The Giant Guards,
whom he had hounded very nearly to death on
so many occasions, fired salvos over his grave.
And those salvos over the grave of Frederick
William I marked the end of one era in Prussian
history and the beginning of another. A young
man who had despised the coarse and often
brutal style of his father, much as Frederick
William had hated the approach to the kingship
of his own parent, had been waiting in the
wings. This young man was, among so many
other things, a poet who, by his own claim,
could write 200 lines of poetry in one hour.
He was now King Frederick II of Prussia. He
was not yet known as "the Great." But that
would come soon enough.

CHAPTER V

THE PHILOSOPHER AS WARRIOR

King Frederick II was born in Berlin
on January 24, 1712. He was the third son
sired by Frederick William I, but was the
only one to survive. The name Frederick was
given him by his grandfather who believed,
perhaps since it was his own name, that the
appellation Frederick had always brought good
luck to the Hohenzollerns.

Frederick's father had first entrusted
the education of his children to French
Huguenots. As a result, Frederick's basic
language came to be French instead of German.
Frederick the Great was, in fact, often heard
to say in later life that he spoke German
like a coachman. When the infant prince
reached his early boyhood years, Frederick
William I added to his tutors one General
von Finckenstein, a veteran soldier of sixty,
and a Colonel Kalkstein, who had often distinguished himself under battle conditions.
By surrounding his son with militarists he
hoped that he might ensure his son's becoming
a militarist.

Frederick William very much desired
that his heir carry on the work in Prussia
that he had begun. Therefore he tried everything he could to make young Frederick into
a carbon copy of himself. The specific object
of Frederick William's plan of instruction
for young Frederick had three aims: (1) his
son was to become a "proper" Christian;
(2) he was to be made into an excellent
administrator; and (3) he was to become an
exemplary soldier. To achieve these ends
Frederick William set up in elaborate detail
a training schedule for his heir. In fact,
the King indicated how his son should spend

every hour of every week. Since Frederick
William had decided that only positive and
useful knowledge be passed on to his son,
he expressly forbade that the young prince
study any subjects he regarded as "useless
or frivolous." Among the subjects forbidden
the young pupil was Latin, perhaps because
it was the traditional language of the scholars
and pedants the King disliked so much. The
core of the young prince's program was to
be practical instruction--arithmetic, the
science of artillery, and political science.
The King saw no use for such things as ancient
history (despite the abundance of military
examples to be found there), and, therefore,
such subjects were forbidden.

Most important, young "Fritz" was
to be taught that his father was his best
friend. Tutors were ordered to use threats
to make the young boy afraid of his mother,
but never his father. To ensure that Fritz
was military-minded, beyond providing him
with the above-mentioned military tutors,
the boy was given a company of children-
soldiers. He was ordered to drill the
uniformed lads regularly. He was also provided
with a model arsenal, fitted with every con-
ceivable weapon of war. When young Frederick
seemed to take a delight in beating
rhythmically on a little drum, the King was
overjoyed. He believed that he had finally
discovered in his son the natural expression
of a warlike instinct.

Despite the careful planning of the
King, however, the education of his son took
a direction quite different from the one
Frederick William had desired. The tutors
followed his instructions to the letter, but
they did not work out the way the monarch
had intended. For example, Frederick's first
tutor in French was one Madame de Rocoulle,
an old French refugee from religious persecu-
tion. She had taught French as a young woman

to King Frederick William I. In fact, she
could speak only French. The result of her
instruction with the King had been that he
had come to detest French culture. Given
his own experience, Frederick William assumed
that it was bound to work out much the same
way with his son. It did not. In fact, young
Fritz not only took the French language as
his own, but he also took up French manners
and culture. Because the young heir often
had to memorize parts of a German catchism
from German hymns as a punishment for something or other he had done, Fritz came to
loathe the German language his father had
intended he prefer over French.

Since Frederick, even as a youngster,
was being shaped in a direction contrary to
his father's wishes, a clash between father
and son was highly likely. The fact that
the conflicts between father and son mentioned
earlier in this book were built into
eighteenth-century royal houses anyway meant
that a clash between this parent and his
offspring was probably inevitable. This
inevitability was heightened by the fact that
young Frederick found little to appeal to
him in his father's Tobacco Parliament, which
he was forced to attend on a regular basis.
Fritz thought the air of the Parliament was
foul, the jokes made there overly coarse,
and the company endured quite boring. He
expressed his distaste and indicated that
he preferred to associate with intellectuals,
to stay in his own rooms to read or play the
flute. To the King's horror, young Fritz
also displayed a dislike for the hunt.
Slaughtering stags or boars was repugnant
to him. He wrote a note to a friend about
this time saying: "I confess to you that
I have no inclination for the hunt. "This
passion is entirely loathsom to me."

These tendencies appearing in his
son were of course, most displeasing to

Frederick William. Even before the young
boy who would be king one day had grown to
manhood his father harbored resentment against
him because he was not sufficiently robust.
The Prussian monarch simply could not bear
the notion that any offspring of his was a
weakling. Frederick William had fond hopes
that a program of exercise would make his
young son strong. Hence, he enforced upon
Fritz a regimen including joining the monarch
in hunting expeditions and upon his trips
through the provinces. So strenuous was all
of this that it often endangered young
Frederick's health.

The coming breach between father and
son was forecast one day when they both were
out on the hunt. It was bitter cold. Young
Fritz had therefore put on gloves to keep
his hands warm. Seeing this, the King angrily
reproached the boy for his weakness in front
of the royal hunting party. Soon after,
Frederick William purposely picked for his
son a horse to ride after the hounds which
was known to be spirited and rebellious. The
animal threw Fritz, injuring his arm. Then,
although the boy had his arm in a sling and
could scarcely walk because of his injuries,
Frederick William made him ride in a ceremony
held on the parade grounds the following day.

The King became increasingly upset
about his son's behavior. He began to believe
that he was raising a French fop to be his
successor. He explained in disgust on one
occasion that: "Fritz is a piper and a
poetaster; he cares nothing about soldiers
and will ruin all that I have done." The
King's resentment deepened when he discovered
that the crown prince had contracted some
debts. This fact no doubt raised visions
in the kingly mind of the profligate spending
of his own father. He therefore began asking

of his advisors: "How can such an extravagant
and wasteful boy be a suitable ruler for my
poor state."

The first overt breach between Fritz
and his father transpired at a dinner party
in 1724. In the company of a considerable
number of people the King said loudly that
Frederick simply did not think as he did.
This unfortunate circumstance, he held, resulted
from the activities of some people, shadows
he did not name, who were trying to put contrary
notions into the lad's head. He then gave
his son a public lecturing on the value of
a good army and keeping plenty of funds on
hand: "Concentrate your efforts on a good
army and on money; for in these two things
lie the glory and security of a ruler." As
he was speaking, to emphasize his points,
he began tapping his son on the cheek, gently
at first. After a bit, however, the taps
became slaps. Finally, a concluding point
was made violently by striking the table so
hard with his fist that he broke several
porcelain plates.

Young Fritz was no fool. He tried
to create a more tolerant atmosphere by writing
his father a letter. That seemingly reasonable
action was to little avail. His parent simply
reproached Fritz for not loving him sufficiently.
His answer was actually a typical variation
on the "Love me, you scum!" approach that
he had used so often on his subjects in the
streets of Berlin. Moreover, he wrote in
his answer to Ftitz's letter:

. . . you know well that I can not bear
an effeminate fellow who has no manly
inclinations; who is shy, can not ride
or shoot, and is not neat in his person;
who has his hair dressed like a fool and
does not have it cut. For all this I
reprimanded you, but in vain. There is

no improvement in anything. . . . I
cannot bear one who is conceited and
over-bearing . . . ; who grimaces as
if he were an idiot and obeys my will
only when he is forced to do so; who
does nothing from motives of love for
his father . . . and is otherwise good
for nothing.

After that, the breach widened; for
the King wanted only complete submission to
his will from his son. Characteristically,
Frederick William believed that he had simply
been too mild in his actions toward his son.
He therefore resorted to sterner methods.
If he discovered Fritz playing his flute,
he would break the flute and cane his son.
If he found the crown prince reading, he would
seize his books and throw them into the fire.
Young Fritz had taken a liking to a three-
pronged silver fork with which he liked to
eat rather than the two-pronged one in common
use at the royal table. The King discovered
Frederick eating with it. His response was
to again beat his son with his cane. Finally,
it became impossible for the crown prince
to enter the presence of his father without
risking a rain of blows on his head. Even
judged by the rough standards of the eighteenth
century, the Prussian King's treatment of
his son can only be described as pathological.

No matter what the King did, however,
young Fritz managed to resist. Not
surprisingly, he came to loathe his father.
In secret letters to his friends he championed
the cause of any person his father had decided
to punish. Gradually, as Fritz's situation
became intolerable to him, this crown prince
began to consider seriously what ways there
might be for him to escape the incessant
punishment he received. In the international
atmosphere caused by a violent Franco-British
reaction to an alliance between Austria and

Spain in 1725, Frederick William first took
the side of France and Britain. The Prussian
King began to talk of a possible double
marriage between the houses of Hohenzollern
and Hanover. Fritz's elder sister Wilhelmina
would by this plan marry the Prince of Wales.
Frederick would take as his bride one of
the daughters of the Prince of Wales, probably
the Princess Amelia. The marital project
would have linked Prussia closely with England
and Austria was aware of that fact. Hence,
the Austrians began to exert as much pressure
as they could on Frederick William to prevent
the dual Prussian-English union. The man
charged with accomplishing this feat was one
Friedrich Heinrich, Count von Seckendorff,
who was sent to live at the Prussian court
in 1726. Thanks to Seckendorff's personal
influence over the Prussian ruler, combined
with his skillful bribery of Frederick
William's advisors, Prussia left the English
orbit and became a member of the rival Austro-
Spanish League. This would have seemed to
have ended Frederick's possibilities of
escaping from his father's draconian discipline
through the device of marriage.

In spite of a basic change in the
diplomatic climate, King Frederick William
still hoped for the double marriage with
England, at least for a time. And as long
as his father hoped, young Fritz still had
hope of escaping from his detested situation.
Seckendorff kept at work, however. Eventually,
the wily Austrian convinced Frederick William
that the English King was not really in earnest
about the suggested marriage. After some
further desultory negotiations, the double
marriage scheme was finally abandoned by both
the British and the Prussians. The dis-
appearance of the possible British escape
avenue forced Frederick, in 1730, to consider
another and more drastic method of escape.
His resolve to find another way out was
quickened at this juncture by a severe caning

his father had given him in front of a group of assembled and embarrassed troops at Mühlberg. That had done it. Frederick decided to leave Prussia for good and his future role as monarch over the state. He would do this by the simple expedient of fleeing to England and throwing himself on the mercy of his relatives there.

* * * * * * * *

The suggestion has often been made that Frederick the Great was very probably a homosexual. This suggestion derives in part from his relationship with Hans Hermann von Katte, a lieutenant in the Potsdam guards who was involved in Frederick's attempts to escape the cruelty his father inflicted upon him. There is, however, no evidence that Frederick and Katte had a homosexual relationship. The rumor probably springs from Frederick's life-long inability to love any woman and his tendencies to bar them from his presence. The notion also derives from his estranged friend Voltaire's claim, of which more is to be said later, that Frederick had had some homosexual relationships with some of his soldiers and pages.

A more likely explanation for Frederick's close relationship with Katte was that Frederick, a naturally affectionate lad, needed a friend upon whom he could lavish his affection. Because of his father's tendencies toward manic brutality, Frederick was cut off from any supporters in Berlin or Potsdam. Katte was a loyal friend of Frederick's own generation. He filled the role of the supporters who were not there.

Katte was a natural companion for a prince like Frederick. He was, by all accounts, an intelligent person. He, like the crown prince, had interests ranging from mathematics to art, and from art to philosophy.

He possessed considerable charm personally as well, although he was quite an ugly young man in appearance.

During 1730, the King had put Fritz under virtual house arrest. Frederick William's displeasure with young Frederick had reached new heights at this juncture. A rumor that his heir wished to escape him and his "love" had reached his ears. The monarch's displeasure was so aroused at this point that he had even replied to a foreign monarchy's request for a portrait of his son with a statement to the effect that he had no such picture, but that it mattered very little for the painting of any common sort of ape would do just as well.

Sometimes at night, when Frederick was under a loose guard in the Potsdam garrison quarters, Katte would secretly sneak into his room and spend an hour or so with him to talk for a time. Apparently, they spoke of religion and philosophy. They also began to hatch plans to extricate Fritz from what was becoming an increasingly intolerable situation. The opportunity for escape finally came on July 15, 1730.

Frederick William had planned a visit to Western Germany. He had decided to take his son with him, if only to keep an eye on the young man. Frederick, for his part, apparently believed that, once he was out of Prussia, he would stand a far better chance to escape to France. The King of France had already told Fritz privately that he would be welcome and safe there. Katte planned to apply for leave and journey from Berlin to join Frederick later. Enthused, Frederick also enlisted a young page named Kieth, who normally rode beside the King's carriage, to take part in the conspiracy.

On August 4, 1730, Fritz was ready
to slip away from his father's train of
carriages just after the cavalcade had entered
Mannheim. During the course of the day, the
crown prince managed to smuggle a note to
Kieth, ordering him to obtain two horses in
Mannheim and have them ready for the next
day. But even as the crown prince
optimistically schemed Kieth had already begun
to crack, surrounded as he was by the omni-
present aura of fear that hung about King
Frederick William I. When the young page
attended church with the King's party, he
was affected so greatly that he fell upon
his knees before the King and confessed
everything.

The Prussian monarch controlled his
rage for a time. He was not in his own domain
where he could do whatever he wished whenever
he desired. For his part, young Frederick
still believed that his plans to escape were
unknown to any save Kieth and himself. He
did notice, however, that his father had become
more than normally sarcastic toward him. And
Fritz became apprehensive when his father
remarked to him, seemingly out of the blue:
"I thought you would be in Paris by now."
The young prince reacted to these surprising
statements on the part of his father by passing
another note to Kieth: "Things look bad.
Arrange for us to get away." But the arrange-
ments were not made and the trip continued
for the puzzled Fritz.

Frederick William managed to control
his famed temper until the party was traveling
down the Rhine by ship. At that point he
lost control. Near Mainz, he suddenly grabbed
his son and hit him in the face with his cane
until blood ran from the royal offspring's
nose. The King cursed Fritz as a deserter
and traitor and, at one point, became so worked
up that he drew his sword with the obvious
intention of skewering his own son. He was

prevented from this only by a high-ranking
officer who threw himself in front of the
prince calling: "Sire kill me, but spare
your son!" Frederick was hurried away from
the fuming monarch who told others to
interrogate this dastardly "Deserter from
the Prussian army."

It was not long before the other
European courts knew that the crown prince
of Prussia was under close arrest. Rumors
circulated that some foreign powers might
even go so far as to send an expeditionary
force to rescue Frederick. To prevent this
from happening, the King ordered the prince
to be taken to Küstrin fortress, east of Berlin.
There he was put under close guard.

Orders came back to Berlin to arrest
Katte. Although Frederick's good friend had
every chance to escape, he did not do so.
No one actually knows why, but Katte remained
in Berlin where he was eventually taken by
the King's men.

Meanwhile, the King returned and
searched Frederick's personal correspondence,
apparently hoping that he would find some
indication that Frederick was conspiring with
foreign powers. Frederick William also became
so angry at Wilhelmina that he seemed about
to have a stroke. Wilhelmina was quite close
to her brother, the heir, and Frederick
William built upon the fact of that relationship to assume that she had been a party to
the escape plot. According to his daughter's
own written testimony, the King at this point
"became black in the face, his eyes sparkling
fire, his mouth foaming." He grabbed his
daughter and hit her several times in the
face with his fist. She fell backward, striking
her head. At least momentarily, she had been
knocked unconscious. There was then much
screaming from the Queen and others in the room

who begged the King not to kick Wilhelmina to death, which he was apparently set upon doing.

These incidents took place in a ground-floor room of the palace. As this was going on, Katte passed by the window under armed escort. The King was told that Katte had arrived. This news distracted him from Wilhelmina. The King said to his distraught family: "Now I shall have proof about that scoundrel Fritz and the scum Wilhelmina, clear proof to cut the heads off both of them."

Frederick William was now prepared to get at the "truth" about how the escape plans were formulated. Apparently he had come to believe that the whole affair had been tied in with some sort of British plot to place Frederick on the throne of Prussia in his place. He therefore was set upon extracting confessions from Katte and his son through torture. Cooler heads prevailed, however, and Frederick William was persuaded not to do as he had threatened. Instead, since he was convinced by his advisors that it would look better to the powers to do it that way, Frederick William appointed a commission to interrogate the crown prince. Frederick did well before the commission, which failed to prove complicity between himself and any foreign power. Then he wrote a humble plea to his father, throwing himself on the monarch's mercy. Frederick William tore up the statement in anger when he received it. He was furious at having failed to trap his son in what he was certain had been a plot with some foreign and antagonistic state scheming to use his own heir against him. In his fury he ordered that he never hear the name of his son again. He further directed that the nature of Fritz's punishment be made more severe.

A court-martial was assembled to try
Katte and Kieth. The court deliberated four
days and then sentenced Katte to life
imprisonment. But the King wanted young Katte
dead. Two of Katte's relatives were field
marshals. The King explained his actions
to those two high-ranking soldiers as follows:
". . . by rights Katte . . . deserves to die
by tearing with red-hot pincers and hanging,
he shall nevertheless . . . be put to death
by the sword."

Frederic William characteristically
supervised personally each detail of Katte's
beheading. He ordered that, once Katte had
been killed, the body and the severed head
be left outside the crown prince's window
for several hours. Frederick was informed
of the nature of his father's plans at five
in the morning, two hours before the execution
was to take place. Emotionally, he pleaded
with his captors to take his life in exchange
for Katte's. At seven in the morning he was
forced by his jailers to go to the window.
Even though Frederick could only see Katte's
walk to the scaffold and not the execution
itself, since the scaffold was obscured from
his view, the experience was too much for
him. He collapsed and remained in a fever
the rest of the day.

* * * * * * * *

Frederick was certain that the King
would have him executed next. By this time,
however, the leading sovereigns and statesmen
of Europe, including the Holy Roman Emperor
himself, had, through their representatives
in Berlin, asked the King to take mercy on
his son. Even the heads of the anti-English
factions at Berlin and the Old Dessauer, who
had never particularly liked Fritz, all asked
that the monarch show mercy to his son.
Frederick William finally came to the conclusion

that it was better not to alienate entirely
the sympathies of the crowned heads of Europe
and the feelings of his own subjects. As
it finally worked out, Frederick William was
satisfied with Frederick's signing a document
giving up his hereditary right to the throne
should he ever so offend his father again.
The King had obviously become calmer. At
about this time he confided to an advisor:
"I hope that he will not end up on the gallows
yet." Thereafter, Frederick was released
from Küstrin prison. He was forced to remain
in town as a mere civilian, to learn as a
junior clerk the business of provincial
administration. In this fashion, Frederick
could simultaneously be punished even as he
was introduced to the practical problems of
government.

On November 20, 1730, Frederick took
up his duties in the local department of war
and agriculture. On Sundays he was forced
to attend three religious services. The only
books Frederick William allowed him to read
were the Bible, the Psalter, and Johann Arndt's
True Christianity. The crown prince's own books
and his writing had fallen into his father's
keeping and were subsequently sold. Fritz
soon wearied of his new existence, not because
he found the nature of his duties so repugnant,
but because his leisure time was so boring
with all his favorite avocations forbidden.

Frederick William paid his son a visit
in August of 1731. He spent most of his time
with his son shouting insults at the crown
prince. But Frederick had learned how to
act in terms of his own survival; as he
listened to the tirade he kissed his father's
feet three different times. Apparently
satisfied with this performance on the part
of his son, Frederick William took his leave.
Remaining behind him were instructions to
relax the restrictions on Fritz. Meanwhile,
back in Berlin, since the discovery of

Frederick's escape plans, his sister Wilhelmina
had been locked up in her rooms and fed on
a diet that was substantially bread and water.
Frederick William told his daughter that she
had a choice; she could marry one of the three
suitors he had rounded up for her or she could
spend the rest of her life imprisoned in a
castle. She was further warned that her
beloved Fritz would never be allowed to leave
Küstrin unless she wedded as her father desired.

Wilhelmina obeyed her father. In
November of 1731 she was married to the
hereditary prince of Bayreuth. The King also
honored an earlier promise he had made that
Frederick would be pardoned if she did as
he had required. Fritz was allowed to return
from exile from Küstrin. Wilhelmina had
certainly not done all of this out of love
for her brother. She was just as anxious
as was Fritz to escape the periodic outbursts
of savagery which typified her father's
behavior.

Frederick's situation bettered rapidly
from that juncture forward. He was reinstated
in the army at the rank of colonel-designate.
The arrangement of the crown prince's marriage
was also an integral part of a bettering
situation for the young man. The Austrians
had convinced Frederick William that Elizabeth
of Brunswick-Bevern, the only Protestant family
closely related to the Habsburgs, would be
a very good mate for the nineteen-year-old
Frederick. This union, it was thought by
the Austrian party at the Prussian court,
would tie the Hohenzollerns and Habsburgs
more closely together. Fritz was willing,
if his father would agree to give him enough
money to keep up an establishment of his own
removed from the King's court. Frederick's
willingness was not based on any liking for
his intended. Her only appeal was that she
offered him greater personal freedom. In
private he told friends that he would prefer

the "greatest whore in Berlin" to this "ugly,
clumsy, and stupid" princess. But marriage
was an escape. He wrote one of his confidants
that, once he was married, and at a reasonable
distance from Berlin and out of his father's
way he would "let Madame go her way and as
far as I am concerned I shall do as I please."

The Queen had her doubts about
Frederick's intended too, calling her "a
proper goose." Princess Charlotte, a younger
sister of the crown prince, evaluated Fritz's
bride-to-be negatively as well: "The other
day I was present at her toilette. She stinks
like the plague. . . . I also noticed that
she is misshapen." The Austrian envoy,
Seckendorff, who had helped arrange the marriage in the first place, wrote back to Vienna
that the rumors of Elizabeth's lack of beauty
were greatly exaggerated by her many
detractors. He pointed out that her many
pimples were bound to disappear, that her
pockmarks would probably fade given time,
that her neck was bound to grow less scrawny,
and, when she had gone through a period of
time as an ugly duckling, that she would
eventually emerge as a beautiful swan.

For his part, Frederick William I
was delighted with the engagement. He was,
however, upset that young Frederick did not
send his "beloved" very many letters. The
King made his displeasure known to Fritz who,
by this time, knew better than to ignore his
father's instructions. The young man
obediently increased the flow of royal mail
to his betrothed. The King took note and
said with considerable satisfaction that he
now knew that "the lovers are thoroughly in
love."

The wedding took place on June 12,
1733. Unlike Frederick William's optimistic
assessment, the young lovers were hardly in
love; for, as soon as the wedding was over,

Frederick spent an hour in bed with his bride.
He then left her, put on his clothes, and
joined the festivities in the palace garden
of the Duke of Wölfenbuttel, the bride's
godfather, whose home had provided the setting
for the royal nuptials. As soon as that social
gathering was over Frederick left for his
regiment. Some historians claim that the
one hour he spent in bed with his new wife
was the only time that Frederick ever spent
there. Whether this is true or not, no one
will probably ever know. The crown prince's
opinion of the wedding and its immediate
aftermath is known, however, As soon as he
had taken leave of Wölfenbuttel, Frederick
sat down to write a ltter to his sister
Wilhelmina. He told her: "Thank God it is
all over."

The end Frederick had sought in marrying
Elizabeth was achieved. Fritz was back in
favor with the King and he had become master
of his own house, a ruined lakeside castle
named Rheinsberg located north of Berlin.
Actually, it was not until the summer of 1736
that the royal couple was able to move into
the palace. Once there, Frederick gathered
around him the kind of friends his father
would never have allowed him in the days before
he had been married. These friends were
cosmopolitan people who could talk books,
poetry, painting, and other similar topics
with Frederick. They provided for him what
his wife never could, the benefits of
intellectual companionship.

As to the relationship between Frederick
and his wife, there really was no relationship.
The crown prince always showed his mate
considerable courtesy. But he never demonstrated any affection toward her. Moreover,
once he became the ruler of Prussia himself,
she was hardly ever allowed in his presence.
The problem was not only that the union between
Fritz and Elizabeth was one of those personal

mismatches for reasons of state which so
clutter the history of som many European
monarchical lines. Elizabeth was a kindly,
if drab, lady who, if she had not been born
to the purple, would very likely have made
some innkeeper an excellent wife. Unfortunately for her, she was wedded to one of the
most brilliant men of the eighteenth century,
a century more typified by brilliant people
than most earlier ones.

The four years spent at Rheinsberg
(1736-1740) may well have been the best of
Frederick's life. At least, he was able to
indulge himself there in the study of classical
French literature, the writings of the great
Greeks and Romans in French translation,
philosophy, and poetry. He also played the
flute as much as he wished and began a correspondence with many of the famous writers he
had long admired, among them the internationally
known French author Voltaire. He was able
at Rheinsberg to spend an incredible amount
of time reading. He also wrote, his most
important piece being the *L'Antimachiavel*, which
was published anonymously in 1740. This work
was a refutation of the cynical Italian's
amoral principles of statecraft. The
Antimachiavel was also an expression of Frederick's
idealism and high moral principles. Of course,
as so many historians have noted, as soon
as Frederick came to the throne he pushed
the high idealism of his book aside and began
to act in terms of dynastic interest and
personal ambition.

The result of the four Rheinsberg
years was to make Frederick into one of the
most cultured and best informed princes of
Europe. If not born to the kingship, Frederick
would certainly have made an excellent scholar
and writer. Through hard study, Frederick
was ready to become ruler when his father
died. When Frederick William did die, the
news shot around Berlin like the signals

issuing from a semaphore. The people generally were relieved and happy. No longer could the avenging angel of the Hohenzollerns roam the streets with his punishing cane. For the whole of the day of Frederick William's death the inhabitants of Berlin cheered and celebrated, embracing one another in the streets. There was a new king in Berlin, a man the French ambassador described as "the prettiest, daintiest Majesty in the world." Actually Frederick was about five feet seven inches in height with curly hair and blue eyes. The French ambassador, after years of Frederick William's coarseness, also noted that Frederick radiated an "irresistible" charm in conversation and demonstrated an attentive intelligence rarely seen in monarchs. Things were bound to be better in Prussia. Of this most of the celebrating Berliners were certain.

* * * * * * *

Perhaps the people of Berlin were overly confident. In truth, no one knew what to expect when the old King died. For the last five years, Frederick had been left completely out of the center of national affairs, rhyming and studying at Rheinsberg. Not only the Berliners were in doubt as to what Frederick's rule might mean. His generals and ministers were similarly dubious. Frederick put these men at ease in his first meeting with them. He thanked them for the "splendid army" they had helped build. he assured them that there would be no personnel changes and that his father's advisors would be his own. Frederick did surprise some, who looked upon him as a mere flutist and essayist, by asserting his authority. He said that he had heard charges against some of those assembled of "undue avarice, harshness, and arrogance" and that he wanted to hear no more of such things.

The general tone of what his rule
would be like was established by King
Frederick II when he did away with much of
the ceremony of previous coronations. His
attitude became plain when he remarked
sarcastically that a crown was "simply a poor
hat which let in the rain." In addition to
these first comments, Frederick's initial
policy declarations established the administrative style of his kingship. He indicated
to his civil servants that they were not to
enrich themselves by exploiting any of his
subjects. He primary aim, he maintained,
was the enrichment of his country. Soon enough,
he proved that his study of Enlightment writers
had left its mark. He issued an edict
abolishing judicial torture, except in extreme
cases where treason and murder were involved.
This act was promulgated over the protests
of his judges who predicted that, in the absence
of proper punishments, every thief and ruffian
in Germany would likely flee to Prussia for
sanctuary. He also did away with the barbarous
practice by which mothers who had killed their
own children were sewn into sacks and drowned.
He issued an edict of religious toleration,
saying that all religions were equally good
and that "everyone must go to heaven" in his
own way. He revived Frederick I's Academy
of Sciences, and added many new impressive
members to it. All of this is impressive,
even in retrospect, making it appear as if
an era of enlightened despotism had indeed
appeared in Prussia.

* * * * * * * *

It must be understood that Frederick
did not impress the other crowned heads of
Europe when he came to the throne, even if
his eventual works make him quite impressive
to us today. He was an unknown quantity.
What was known of him, the idea that he was
a poet-king, hardly inspired awe. Moreover,

he was Frederick William's son. And that
monarch's antics had made him a standing joke
among European rulers. Because Frederick
William had seemed such a joke to them, because
he had never used against them the excellent
army he had built up, these rulers had a number
of times betrayed the Prussian ruler and broken
alliances with him. In fact, the court of
the Hohenzollerns under Frederick William
had seemed so ridiculous to the rest of Europe
that one Baron Böllnitz had handsomely supple-
mented his personal income by circulating
accounts of Frederick William's actions in
a kind of newsletter, which could be had for
a fee, among the various European courts.
Frederick II, however, was not for long taken
as lightly as had been his father among the
councils of Europe.

Five months after Frederick became
King of Prussia, Emperor Charles VI of Austria
died on October 20, 1740. His death was sudden
and unexpected. He left behind him a daughter,
Maria Theresa, but there was no male heir.
Because a woman had never ruled in Austria
in the way one had in England or Sweden,
Charles VI spent the last years of his rule
trying to make certain that his duaghter's
succession to the throne would be recognized
by all the important monarchs. To ensure
this, he had drawn up the so-called "Pragmatic
Sanction." This document was then agreed
to by all the important crowned heads, including
Frederick William I of Prussia. Despite the
existence of the signed Pragmatic Sanction,
however, as soon as Charles of Austria died,
several princes, giving one excuse or another,
said that they would not recognize Maria
Theresa's right to take the crown for herself.
The ruler of Bavaria moved first by having
himself elected Holy Roman Emperor in 1742,
since Maria Theresa, because of her gender,
could not fill that traditional Habsburg post.
Perhaps more important, the Bavarian ruler
laid claim to some Habsburg territories, which

started the other powers to doing much the same sort of thing. Frederick II, for his part, decided to use this opportunity to seize Silesia.

Frederick's motives at this juncture were, as one might expect from this complex man, numerous and diverse. Prussia had long been typified by the holding of vast stretches of only relatively productive lands. Silesia was the Habsburgs' richest province, a land of lush farms, vast underground deposits of minerals, particularly coal. Moreover, it was a land of prosperous cities. In addition to its obvious material assets, Silesia provided for Frederick a chance to take his revenge on Austria for having duped his father so many times. It was, for instance, known to Frederick that Seckendorff had, even as he had maneuvered Frederick William I, reported in secret back to Vienna that Frederick William was a coward, afraid to stand up and fight. Frederick knew that Prussia was still seen in this vein by the other powers. The young ruler of Prussia wanted very much to reverse that broadly accepted judgment about his state. He burned with a fierce desire to win glory for his state and for himself. Lastly, from a purely pragmatic point of view, it was a good time to make the move against the Austrians. England had been at war with Spain since 1739. It was reasonable to assume that, given the long-standing enmity between the French Bourbons and the Austrian Habsburgs, Frederick would be able to secure France as an ally while Austria would have to stand with England. And it was assumed by the King of Prussia that England would be too busy elsewhere to make very much of a commitment to Maria Theresa.

Frederick's legal experts provided their King with a justification for his attack on Silesia. This was very likely an academic exercise in that the ruler of Prussia was set on launching his war of conquest anyway. Nevertheless, Frederick did have an opportunity to make good a claim that the Hohenzollerns had long had to a half-dozen small counties in Silesia. In fact, what his legal experts provided for Frederick was a claim based on a pact concluded some 400 years earlier. This pact had long since lost any meaning it had ever had. As far as the legal demand was concerned, Frederick was not overly concerned with its details. He instructed his Foreign Minister as follows: "The legal question is an affair for you ministers, and it is time to work it up secretly, for the orders to the troops have been issued."

When it became apparent that Prussian troops were massing at the border of Silesia, Maria Theresa instructed her representatives in Berlin to discover what was intended by such actions. No one was able to find out for her as this particular state secret was closely guarded. Frederick kept even his own ministers from discovering the details of his plans. By mid-December of 1740, Prussian columns were marching toward Silesia.

The superb war machine that Frederick William and the Old Dessauer had put together was now moving along the muddy bogs that the roads of Silesia had become during the wet December. Resistance never appeared. Three towns attempted to make a stand. These were bypassed and cut off. On January 1, 1741, Breslau, the capital of Silesia, was taken. Up to that point, not a single shot had been fired. In fact, the city of Breslau simply opened wide its gates in response to King Frederick II's promise of religious toleration. When the Prussian ruler rode into the Silesian capital he was cheered wildly by the local inhabitants. "I never saw such enthusiasm," wrote one observer back to Prussia.

95

The Austrians had been taken by
surprise. Quickly, the Habsburgs generals
got busy mobilizing a force of 15,000 men
under one Adam von Neipperg. By April of
1741, Austrian troops were filtering across
the mountain passes from Bohemia into Silesia.
The two armies first met at Mollwitz. Even
though the better trained and armed force,
the Prussians were green troops as far as
real battle was concerned, for it must be
remembered that the Garrison King had kept
his state at peace. The Prussian soldiers
therefore became overly nervous and fired
too soon. Eventually, they became so dis-
organized and so badly confused that some
of them were even firing into their own lines.
Frederick was on the field of battle himself.
He rode back and forth, trying, even though
new to combat, to extricate his men from the
mess into which they had fallen. Finally,
his generals convinced him to ride to the
rear. After he had left the field, his
commander, Kurt von Schwerin, relieved of
the responsibility of looking out for his
monarch, reassembled the troops. In the mean-
time, the Austrian cavalry had managed to
get itself stuck in a marsh.

Schwerin was able to reassemble and
unleash the perfected weapon that was the
Prussian grenadiers. Soldiers like these
had not been seen in Europe before. A defeated
Austrian officer commented admiringly later:

> I hever saw anyting more beautiful.
> They marched with the utmost composure,
> arrow-straight, their front like a
> plumb-line, absolutely level, as if
> they had been on parade. . . .

Mollwitz was turned by these grenadiers from
a defeat into a victory. After eight hours,
the Austrians fled the scene in terror.

The smashing Prussian victory at Mollwitz surprised all of Europe. It had been generally expected that the Austrians would punish Frederick for his treacherous attack. Given the political moralities of the time, the next move on the part of the powers was to have been expected; France quickly attempted to take advantage of Habsburg weakness by entering on Frederick's side as did Bavaria. Earlier, some of the other German states, most importantly Saxony and Hanover, had sized up Prussia's chances and, expecting their neighbor to lose, had quickly opted for the Habsburgs. Hence, the fighting spread quickly.

Strengthened by the French-Bavarian intervention, Frederick was able to sign a treaty with the Austrians on October 9, 1741. By it, he was given most of Silesia. The agreement was to be kept secret to hide the fact that, having gotten various powers into a war against the Austrians, he was now leaving them in the lurch. Thus was ended successfully for the Prussians what is called in German history "The First Silesian War." However, the general European War of the Austrian Succession, initially sparked by his invasion of Silesia, was continued by the other combatants until 1748.

Freed from the Prussian pressure in Silesia, the Austrians drove the French and Bavarians out of Bohemia. Beating the French decisely must have inspired Marie Theresa, or so it appeared to Frederick. The King of Prussia came to believe that, thus inspired, the Habsubrgs might be ready to attempt the regaining of Silesia. The Prussian ruler decided, therefore, that he would launch a preventive war to keep the Austrians from retaking his new province. At the head of his troops, Frederick won brilliant victories in this "Second Silesian War" of 1744-1745. At Hohenbriedberg some 40,000 Prussians had

completely routed a larger Austrian-Saxon
force oof 58,000. The many-sided Prussian
ruler celebrated his event by composing the
"Hohenfriedberg March." This piece of music
was sufficiently well done that it became
a permanently popular piece of martial music
in Germany thereafter. After more victories,
Maria Theresa again acknowledged that
Frederick was the "rightful" ruler of Silesia.
The Second Silesian War came to a halt and
once again Frederick had proven the superiority of the Prussian army.

During the next ten years, both
Frederick and Maria Theresa enlarged their
armies. Most important, the Habsburgs used
this decade of peace to make new secret
alliances (Russia and Saxony). They also
launched the so-called "Diplomatic Revolution
of the Eighteenth Century" whereby France
replaced England as Austria's ally. This
involved a classic reversal in that these
two powers previously had been deadly enemies
for much of the modern era. As Frederick
became aware of this ominous shift in alliances
through his extensive spy network, he looked
around him to see a combination of enemies
who had either already allied themselves against
Prussia or were getting ready to do so. Yet,
Frederick had never lost even one battle.
This fact tended to make him over-confident.
He expressed his feelings of boundless con-
fidence to Schwerin and also to his younger
brother when he wrote to Prince Henry:
"Prussian officers who have been through our
wars know that neither numbers nor difficulties
could rob us of victory. . . ." Supremely
self-assured, he began a war he felt certain
he was to win.

In August of 1756, Frederick II opened
the Third Silesian War by an unsuccessful
attempt to strike into Bohemia through Saxony.
The protracted struggle that followed, in
the wider European context, is known as the

Seven Years' War. This war was fought all over Europe and on the high seas. As one historian has it, because of this war, in the colonies, "red men scalped each other by the Great Lakes of North America." During the conflict, Frederick had to face the greater share of the European powers, almost single-handed. For a long time, his only meaningful ally was England. To make matters worse, the English gave little effective support. The Prussian monarch won many brilliant victories over French, Austrian and various German forces. Eventually, however, the numerical odds mounted against him until it appeared to them he might well become one of those unlucky generals who "won all the battles only to lose the war." By 1758-1759, the Russians were marching through East Prussia and slaughtering thousands off Prussian soldiers. At this point, Frederick's prospects seemed to be so dark that the King commonly took with him a vial of poison secreted on his person so that no one might take the King of Prussia alive. By his own admission, he fingered that vial more than once in the face of near disaster.

Frederick survived all of this, however, and finally a stroke of luck came to him in 1762. Empress Elizabeth off Russia hated Frederick passionately. Perhaps she detested him with good cause; for the Prussian ruler had once called her one of the "three whores" who ruled Europe (Maria Theresa and Madame Marquise de Pompadour, the mistress of King Louis XV of France being the other two). He also had suggested in his caustic way that Elizabeth fornicated with her Cossack Guards as a regular pastime. But to Frederick's immense good fortune the Russian's female ruler died suddenly as the end result of a life of drunkenness and debauchery on January 5, 1762. Peter III then came to the throne of Russia. The new Russian Tsar was a devoted admirer of the Prussian monarch.

Out of his seemingly limitless admiration
for the man who was probably Europe's most
brilliant ruler Peter promptly withdrew his
forces from the war. By July 9, 1762,
however, Peter was assassinated and replaced
by his wife, Catherine the Great. Frederick
hastened to keep the good relationship with
the wife that he had had with her husband
and Russia did not reenter the war against
him.

The truth was that Austria was nearly
as exhausted as Prussia by 1762. The
Habsburg's chief ally, France, had been
defeated almost everywhere by England. Maria
Theresa gave up at last any hope of reconquer-
ing Silesia. Peace was concluded on
February 15, 1763. Frederick returned to
Prussia, tired and sick to death of war. In
his own words he was: "gray as a jackass.
Every few days, it seems, I lose another tooth
and I am half lame with gout." And thus this
exhausted man came home, miserable and yet
victorious, while all over Europe he was now
known as "The Great."

* * * * * * *

Through his victories in the Silesian
wars, often against seemingly impossible odds,
Frederick had proven himself to be a military
genius. An effigy of Frederick the Great
was paraded through the streets of London
while large crowds shouted "Hosanna!" in his
praise as though he were Christ himself. In
Italy he was venerated in the manner of a
saint of the church. The few Prussian travelers
abroad as far south as Sicily were inundated
with offers of jugs of wine and baskets of
fruit. All across Europe Frederick was honored
or feared. Not only had he prevailed against
enormous odds, he had also won out again and
again over the house of Habsburg, a ruling
house which was in the mind of many Europeans

a long-time international bad boy and thus
hated by many. Moreover, because of the three
Silesian wars, he had helped most Germans,
not just Prussians, to overcome a kind of
broad-based, traditional inferiority complex
from which they had suffered since the era
of the Thirty Years' War; for that great and
long conflict had humiliated Germans generally
as their land became the bloodstained cockpit
for other nations. By his brilliant victories,
Frederick had stimulated in some an awakening
national awareness based on a kind of Germanic
pride. A full-blow nationalism would emerge
from this and other sources during the
Napoleonic period at the beginning of the
nineteenth century.

Despite the fact that he was being
lionized across Europe, however, Frederick
had returned to Berlin in 1763, saddened by
the strains placed on his kingdom by a long
and enervating conflict. He had been very
close to disaster in the Seven Years' War
when, at one time, the armies of Prussia had
been forced to fight on three separate fronts
against Austria, Russia, and France together
with their various German allies. He had
therefore come to realize just how precarious
the position of Prussia was between three
continental great powers--Russia, Austria,
and France. He believed that another general
war might well bring to Prussia the disaster
she had just narrowly escaped. Therefore,
after 1963, the same Frederick who had been
so willing to go to war in 1740 became a
champion of peace and the defender of the
status quo. It was Catherine II of Russia
and Joseph II of Austria who acted as the
ambitious heads of state after 1763. Once
the aggressor, it was Frederick's turn to
hold these two monarchs in check through a
combined policy of diplomacy and a show of
force.

Conscious of the continued threats
to the long-exposed, and straggling frontier
of Prussia and constantly aware of how close
he had come to disaster in 1762, Frederick
decided to guarantee the survival of his
kingdom. In his view, this could be done
only by maintaining on a permanent wartime
footing a large standing army at a strength
of some 150,000 men. He thus decided to follow
his father's example rather than that of the
Great Elector. The Great Elector, as soon
as the First Northern War had ended, had at
once reduced his forces to a peacetime footing.
He had done the same thing in 1679 at the
end of the Franco-Swedish War. But Frederick's
father, the Garrison King, had always included
in his policies the idea of constantly building
up the army. Frederick followed the way of
his father. From the end of the Seven Years'
War some two-thirds of the Prussian national
income went to the army. Every sixth man
in the kingdom was under arms. France was
far richer and larger than Prussia, but Prussia
had an army that was almost the size of
France's. Moreover, the building up of the
strength of the army was followed by the
creation of many new fortresses.

Frederick now purged his officers
corps of non-nobles, believing that officers
drawn from the bourgeoisie did not have a
sufficient "sense of honor" to serve in the
higher ranks. The reason for purging the
middle-class officers has been put a bit
differently in Gordon Craig's *The Policies of the
Prussian Army*. Craig has written that the
bourgeoisie had to be removed from the officer
corps because they were driven, in Frederick
the Great's view, "by material rather than
moral considerations" and were "too rational
in moments of disaster to regard sacrifice
as either necessary or commendable."
Frederick believed that he simply could not
have that sort of attitude among his officers.
In the King's view it was only the sacrifice

of all personal goals, the subordination of individual interests to the great good of the state, that had saved Prussia in impossible circumstances. In this way the kingdom became a military state wherein the army and government were nearly one and the same, where most of the administrators, as was the King himself, were also basically soldiers.

Whether Frederick was actually in sufficient danger after 1763 to justify a standing army of such size and the establishment of such a militarized state has been argued by historians. Some have pointed out that Frederick was in no real danger from France or Britain, who were both more intent upon ruining each other. Austria was nearly as exhausted as Prussia for some years after the end of the Third Silesian War and Poland was widely known to be powerless. Only the restlessness of Russia under Catherine II seemed a problem. But Catherine II of Russia readily accepted Frederick's offer of friendship. Whether or not Frederick should have reduced the military establishment, given the international situation in 1763, can be argued pro and con. It is harder, however, to argue against another assertion growing out of his army policies; it is held by almost everyone who has written about it that his maintenance of the policies of his father firmly established the military tradition in the Prussian state so that it was a permanent fixture by the time of his death.

Thus, after 1763, the foreign policy of Frederick the Great was dominated by the quest for security. Prussia simply could not afford another war. The Prussian King had to approach the Tsarita of Russia to win her friendship without binding himself in an alliance which would force him into another war. He managed to do this over the Polish issue.

Catherine II was willing to accept Frederick as an ally only if he would go along with her aggressive policy toward Poland, which had been used as an advanced base by the Russians during the previous war and which had a populace that was thus now accustomed to occupation by Russian troops. Frederick was really less than enthusiastic about allying with the Russians to establish them permanently in Poland. But he hoped by this policy to restrain Catherine's venturesomeness. Moreover, Poland as it was constituted formed something of a power vacuum in Europe. In fact, Poland had been growing progressively more impotent for the past century. The Polish nobility had become so independent that the monarch's power there was a mere shadow of real control. The nobility's embarking in Poland upon a fanatical program of oppressing religious dissidents offered Catherine and Frederick a pretext to intervene there on the behalf of these people, Protestants and Greek Orthodox Catholics, who were their coreligionists.

When the Polish ruler, Augustus III, died in October of 1763, the situation there reached a boiling point. Catherine of Russia desired that a former lover of hers, one Stanilas Poniatowski, be put on the throne. It was her belief that she could control this man who had been so close to her once he was the King of Poland. Frederick II found that the easiest way to win Catherine's friendship was to support her candidate. In April of 1764, Frederick signed with Catherine a defensive alliance, which eventually was extended to 1780. It was agreed at that time that the two monarchs would back the election of Poniatowski and protest the religious dissidents. At the same time, the two also agreed, somewhat cynically, that they would prevent any reforms initiated in the Policy state which might strengthen it and reverse its tendencies toward internal disintegration.

The election of Poniatowski was
accomplished with relative ease, the 50,000
Russian troops on the frontiers of Poland
and considerable funds lavished by Catherine
on the electors being the decisive factors.
For Poland, it was a remarkably peaceful
election in that usually violent land in that,
as one observer put it: "Only ten men were
killed." Soon enough, however, Catherine's
ex-lover showed a taste for independence of
Russian control. Poniatowski launched a policy
aimed at strengthening his chaotic state.
Catherine's reaction to her puppet's rebellion
was to make trouble for him. She helped the
always recalcitrant Polish nobles to set up
a "Confederation" against their ruler. In
1768 she sent in her troops to support the
Confederation. When these Russian soldiers
marched over a bit of Turkish territory on
their way into Poland, it sparked a six-year
war between Russia and Turkey. In the now-
conservative Frederick's view Catherine's
policies were unduly impulsive. But he did
not object as continued friendship with Russia
was still most important to him.

The war with Turkey was an overwhelming
success for Catherine on both land and sea.
Russia had made considerable territorial gains
in the area of the Danube. Both France and
Austria disliked the size of the Tsarita's
new acquisitions. The Bourbons and Habsburgs
both believed that Russia ought to give up
her Danubian prizes and compensate itself
in Poland. However, such a move on the part
of Russia would pose a danger to Austria and
Prussia if not hedged about with certain safe-
guards. It was therefore decided that those
two powers should be compensated elsewhere
in Poland to preserve the existing balance
of power in Europe. The result of negotiations
in which these ideas were discussed between
Russia and Prussia was the First Partition
of Poland in 1772.

Catherine took White Russia and
Lithuania. Maria Theresa, shedding crocodile
tears over her inability to prevent partition,
took Galicia. This profuse weeping followed
by the Austrian annexation of Polish territory, when Frederick the Great heard of
it, caused him to make a typically cynical
remark to the effect that the Habsburg ruler
kept crying while she kept on taking. For
his part, Frederick had few qualms about taking
West Prussia from Poland. His share was only
one-third the size of Catherine's and considerably smaller than Maria Theresa's, but
it was politically more important than either
of theirs. It tied together finally the
central and eastern wings of Prussia and
increased its population by 600,000 people,
many of them Germans.

* * * * * * * *

Joseph II had become the Emperor of
the Holy Roman Empire and joint ruler with
his mother, Maria Theresa, in Austria during
1765. He brought to the Habsburg throne a
new burst of enthusiasm which was personified
in his eager desire to strengthen the Habsburg
holdings. In 1778, the Elector of Bavaria
died without direct heirs. Joseph tried to
use this opportunity to claim a third of
Bavaria for himself. Frederick immediately
opposed Joseph, saying that the status quo
in Germany would be upset by this expansion
of Habsburg holdings. The Prussian ruler
then demanded that Joseph withdraw his troops
from Bavaria. Joseph ignored the demands.
Frederick then sent a Prussian army into
Bohemia to underline his demands. Both
Prussians, with the onset of winter, then
withdrew into Silesia. The soldiers' main
occupation during all of this had been the
finding of enough to eat while on the march.
Since the staple of their diet was potatoes,
they derisively called this conflict, or

near-conflict, the "Potato War." The following
year a treaty was signed and Austria withdrew
from nearly all of the Bavarian territory
it had occupied as a result of its terms.
Frederick had succeeded. The growth of
Habsburg power was avoided.

In 1780, with the death of Maria
Theresa, Joseph II became sole ruler of Austria.
Freed of whatever restraints his mother might
have imposed upon him, Joseph II once again
began putting pressure on neighboring Bavaria.
Once again Frederick opposed him, this time
by forming a League of Princes (the *Fürstenbund*).
The League was eventually joined by seventeen
powers, large and small, both Protestant and
Catholic. Its major purpose was in line with
Frederick's basic policy of preserving the
status quo and Joseph recognized its potential
strength by withdrawing again his claims on
Bavaria. The creation of the *Fürstenbund* was
Frederick's final diplomatic success.

Although he had suffered from gout
for years, severe illness had always been
spared Frederick. In his last years, however,
a host of ailments began to trouble him. But
he still kept to the affairs of state with
iron self-discipline. One of his last acts
was the conclusion of a trade agreement with
the infant United States of America through
its representative, Benjamin Franklin.

Frederick the Great died on August 18,
1786. His last words, naturally enough since
it was the only language he used, were in
French. He referred to himself as "the
mountain" which was passing on. His valet
prepared the corpse and the body was marched
through the streets soon after. The people
were silent. In fact, some may have rejoiced
because in his later years some of the government's economic policies had been unpopular.
At any rate, after lying in state at Potsdam
for a single day his body was transferred

to the valut of the Garrison Church there.
In the vault it was placed next to the coffin
in which his father had been interred.
Ironically, Frederick was scheduled by the
Prussians to spend eternity in death beside
that parent with whom he had so often clashed
in life.

CHAPTER VI

THE PRUSSIAN ABSOLUTIST STYLE

The political life of the seventeenth century had been dominated in Europe by wars, many of them civil conflicts. The worst, but not the only severe internal struggle, had been the Thirty Years' War. These struggles had forced states to hard tests of survival. Moreover, they demanded much money. Therefore, such conflicts tended to force rulers to find every possible way to increase taxes and to enforce their policy decisions upon the subjects within their lands. However, the ever increasing demands on subjects for funds and the Kings' efforts to enforce their will, as was the case with the Brandenburg-Prussian nobility during the Great Elector's reign, caused recalcitrant nobles and others to participate in rebellions. The monarchs' response to rebellion during that century was therefore to continue a centuries-old process of political centralization. The Kings' aim was to rule more effectively by dint of their sole authority, without the participation of subjects except in an advisory capacity. This kind of government, in which the monarch became the solitary power in the state, came to be called absolutism.

By the end of the seventeenth and the beginning of the eighteenth century, most European states, and Brandenburg-Prussia was no exception, had been confronted with a choice between certail "liberties" enjoyed by nobles and the leaders of towns, liberties accompanied by disorder, civil strife and havoc, on the one hand, and a high degree of central control, often intertwined with tyranny, on the other.

109

The choice that had been made in most European states was for absolute monarchy. In this system, normally, the sovereign power in the kingdom was vested in a king, who usually claimed to rule by divine right. This triumph of monarchical power had been won through struggle. In France, for instance, nobles had tenaciously resisted royal encroachments upon the prerogatives traditionally theirs until their revolts were finally crushed. The end result of such struggles was that absolute monarchy was the most widely accepted form of government. And most people were content with it because, compared to the chaotic civil struggles which had preceded it, absolutism seemed an ideally stable form of government. Indeed, it appeared to most people to provide far more security than the systems that had allowed Europe to slip into the savagery of the Thirty Years' War.

Absolutism had many flaws, however. For one thing, absolutist states seemed constantly to be fighting each other as ambitious kings plunged Europe into war to satisfy their vanities or advance the claims of their dynasties. Another obvious defect of absolutism was the fact that it was a workable and successful system if the monarch was equal to its challenges, as in the case of Frederick the Great. But absolutism did not work at all well in the hands of an ineffectual ruler. There were many seventeenth century political thinkers, like the Englishman Thomas Hobbes (1588-1679), who had witnessed the evils loosed upon society during the religious civil wars. Such thinkers declared that people were only safe and happy when their king had sufficient power to maintain order and could pass that power through primogeniture on to his successor. Since absolute government appeared to have the qualifications required, thinkers like Hobbes praised it as the best form of government.

110

those who followed Hobbes, and others who
reached similar conclusions on their own,
forgot that the best can be corrupted and,
when corrupted, becomes the worst. Hence,
under a talented ruler an absolute monarchy
might perform admirably. Under a bad king
its performance would likely prove to be
execrable. Since the king in this sort of
system was answerable to God alone, his subjects
had no legal redress against him for injuries
done to them. Moreover, since the king was
so absolutely in control, the absolutist style
of his state would greatly reflect his own
personality. There were therefore as many
absolutisms as there were kings. But there
was one particular model for most absolutists,
and it had been established in the French
monarchy. The archetype of French absolutism
was Louis XIV.

* * * * * * * *

Louis XIV reigned in France from 1643
to 1715. The general state of Europe in his
day was distinctly favorable to the establishment of the kind of regime he built. Years
of civil and religious discord had created
a deep-seated longing in the people of Europe
for quiet and order. Louis' absolutism was
the shaper of a regime which elevated itself
above the quarrelsome factions of that day
to become the master of the state.

Louis himself seemed to be the ideal
person to become the most absolute of the
absolutists. He sincerely believed himself
to have been chosen directly by God to guide
the destinies of France. The multitude of
details of the kingly trade engrossed him
and, for over fifty years, he kept at the
exacting role for which he believed himself
destined. During his rule, France owned
roughtly one-fifth the population of Europe.

Moreover, France was the most powerful European state and often acted as the arbiter of Europe. Because of this situation, Louis was bound to become a model for the other absolutists of Europe. We have already seen in these pages how Frederick I of Prussia imitated Louis. And Frederick I was certainly not the only one. In sum, simply because he ruled the most powerful state and because his authority was most extensive and absolute of any contemporary monarch, Louis was bound to be aped by crowned heads petty and great all over Europe.

Unfortunately for the people who lived under those who tried to copy Louis, the "Grand Monarch" of France exalted his own personal glory. He considered himself the source of all radiance and light; his symbol was the rising sun. The whole French state was constituted according to a maximum that he himself probably never uttered (it was invented for him later by Voltaire). But Louis might as well have said *"L'etat c'est moi"* (I am the state!); for it personified the character of his reign. In other words, Louis' will was law. He took relatively little interest in the well-being of his subjects. Instead, he exhausted them by long wars and heavy taxation. The nature of Louis' absolutism is probably nowhere better illustrated than in his creation of what some historians have called "The Versailles System."

French kings had traditionally held their courts in the Louvre, close by the Seine. But Louis XIV never liked Paris. He remembered well the disorders of his childhood; during a period of civil war, the capital of France had been a place of fear even for members of the royal family. When he became king, therefore, he moved his residence to the town of Versailles, a hamlet some eleven miles from Paris. There he constructed a palace and gardens so vast that they were wondered

at all over Europe. His Versailles project
was so costly that the expense has been
calculated at the equivalent of hundreds of
millions of dollars in terms of modern currency.
We will never know precisely the amount
expended, however, because Louis ordered the
accounts where that sum was recorded destroyed
on completion of his ambitious project.

Versailles was supplied with water
pumped from a nearby canal to fuel its famous
fountains. The palace was surrounded by
manicured hedges, arbors, gardens, and shaded
walks. The building itself contained a chapel,
a theater, a "marble court," glittering
galleries, sumptuous apartments for the ruler
and his guests, and long connecting halls
tying it all together.

What came to exist at Versailles was
an enormous chateau which normally had 10,000
inhabitants. Six out of every ten francs
collected in French taxes went to support this
glittering centerpiece of absolutism. Moreover,
Versailles was something more than just a
seat of government. It was a place where
every courtier had to go and live, even if
he had to mortgage his estate to do so, if
he was to stand a chance of securing favors
from the sun king. For those who gathered
at the court, court etiquette became a life
study. For example, it was the height of
bad manners at Versailles to knock at a door.
One had to scratch at a door with the little
finger of the left hand, growing the finger-
nail longer to make that act easier.
Precedence was of greatest importance.
Depending on rank, which ran all the way from
the king at the apex to the most lowly courtier
at the bottom of the social pyramid, with
dukes, counts, marquises and barons residing
at various levels, some people were not allowed
to sit in the presence of others. Precedence
among all these rankings became so important

at Versailles that it got to the point where
two prominent people could not meet without
a kind of skirmishing to see who might sit
in the presence of whom. In this kind of
world, it was determined that the most favored
courtier of the day would be allowed to hold
a candlestick while Louis made ready for bed.
It was even considered a mark of distinction
for a designated courtier to fetch the royal
chamberpot.

Louis had made himself into the high
priest of his own cult of majesty at Versailles.
He had convinced his courtiers, the descendants
of those fierce men who had once rebelled
against the crown in that great civil war
of Louis' minority called the Fronde, that
life away from Versailles as "a living death."
If a noble displeased him, the King might
banish the man to his country estate. Out
of favor, that unfortunate might spend the
rest of his days petitioning friends at court
to get him back on the inside of things. Greed
was a potent incentive to remain close to
Louis. Only those who seized and held the
ruler's attention could hope to profit by
his generosity. For Louis, the Versailles
system was an ongoing means by which he could
continuously humiliate and keep low the once-
rebellious and once-haughty nobles of France.

Keeping 10,000 people at Versailles
and fighting the continuous wars of aggrandize-
ment which so typified Louis XIV's rule in
France tended to be quite expensive. The
fiscal system of France that was devised to
provide the funds for all of this was particularly vicious. The means of securing
tax money seemed to have been designed to
ensure a minimum return to the monarch at
a maximum price to his subjects. The heaviest
share of taxes always fell on those least
capable of paying. The clergy, the nobles,
and a vast horde of government officials

were exempt from all forms of direct taxation. It is said that Louis XIV eventually came to realize how the Versailles system and his nearly constant wars to gain glory had exhausted the state and impoverished his people. As he lay dying, having lived longer than both his son and his grandson, he told his great-gradson who was but five years of age (Louis XV):

> My child, you are going to be a great king. Do not imitate me in my taste for building, nor in my love of war. Strive, on the contrary, to live in peace with your neighbors. . . . Make it your endeavor to ease the burden of the people, which I, unhappily, have not been able to do.

Louis XV was too young to understand the exhortation of the dying old king. He never learned the lesson intended by his predecessor when Louis XIV had told him to ease the oppressive burden on the people. Louis XV (1715-1774) lived extravagantly and let his mistress, Madame de Pompadour, have very great influence over his policies. His successor, Louis XVI, was a poor ruler and allowed his wife, Marie Antoinette, to carry on the extravagances of the Versailles system. Most of all, under Louis XIV and his successors, the eleven miles between Versailles and Paris came to represent a great gulf of indifference standing between those who were governed and those who did the governing in France. One reported incident from the life of Marie Antoinette reveals the depth of the gulf described. It was the custom of the queen to ride in her carriage with its windows shuttered when she went into Paris; for she did not like to disturb herself by looking out upon the squalor of the Parisian streets. On one occasion she arrived back to Versailles

from such a visit and expressed great dismay
that there was garbage stuck to the wheels
of the royal vehicle. She demonstrated much
amazement that the wheels were so adorned
and asked in wonderment where such horrible
stuff had been encountered. Apparently, Marie
Antoinette was absolutely ignorant of the
fact that the streets of Paris over which
she had ridden "with blinders on" were, in
her day, customarily full of refuse and strewn
with rotten heaps of offal. In her way, Marie
Antoinette, who would one day lose her head
in the revolutionary turmoil of 1793, was
one of the last and most ridiculous products
of the Versailles system.

* * * * * * * *

This digression into the history of
the French monarchy has been offered in these
pages to serve as a counterpoint to the
Prussian absolutist style of the eighteenth
century. It has already been demonstrated
in these pages that the court of Frederick
William I was a direct contrast to the French
monarchical style typified by vast spending,
pomp and artificial glitter. Moreover, half-
mad as he seemed to be, the Garrison King
believed deeply in his obligation to the
Prussian state, in the code of duty and honor
which bound the King of Prussia. Similarly,
the rule of Frederick the Great also provided
an extreme contrast to the French style of
absolutism.

Under the Austrians, for example,
Silesia had seldom seen the Habsburg ruler.
In fact, when Frederick came to rule that
territory after the First Silesian War, no
Habsburg had visited the province in 150 years.
In contrast, Frederick II went there once
or twice every year, remaining two weeks each
time. In fact, he did this with all of his

provinces. Each of these visits turned out to be a time for hard work. Frederick would take with him a thick leather notebook crammed with statistics about the previous year's crops. He would consult with agricultural managers concerning their yields. He would walk through muddy fields and talk to the peasants as they worked. He checked every bureaucrat who worked anywhere in the local Prussian bureaucracy.

To accomplish so much, Frederick II rose at either three or four o'clock in the morning, after five or six hours of sleep. He then launched into his mountains of correspondence. He did not spend much time getting dressed for the day ahead. Each morning he dressed in the same worn, mended and stained uniform. He finally took a break from correspondence, reports from generals, and petitions from commoners about nine in the morning. Then he played his flute for an hour or so. That process, he held, helped him to think. Then it was back to conferences again as one after another of his councilors appeared to get the monarch's decision on various matters of government. From ten to eleven, Frederick received people in audience. Foreign visitors never ceased to be amazed at seeing shabby common folk peering in the palace windows, hoping to see the King, perhaps trying to have a few words with him. Even more amazing to foreigners was the fact that these commoners were quite commonly successful in their attempts to speak with Frederick the Great. At eleven, the ruler of Prussia personally drilled the guards from horseback. At twelve he lunched. Since lunch was his main meal of the day he might well be surrounded with guests for two or more hours. After lunch, he played the flute for half an hour and then signed letters he had dictated earlier. Then there was reading, more flute in concert with others, and eventually supper late at night.

As Frederick grew older, his very accessibility prompted a great deal of respect from his subjects, although he was not the type of ruler one's people loved. But he was not remote as were other kings. He dressed in austere simplicity. He seemed to incorporate the homespun Germanic ideals of hard work, simplicity and directness of speech. He became that seemingly tritest of proverbial sayings; he was "a legend in his own time." There were literally hundreds of anecdotes constantly circulating about him. He had a caustic wit that shocked many people. But he had a sense of justice that delighted even those who were shocked. One story about Frederick well illustrates the point. A cavalry man had been convicted of having committed sodomy with his horse. The traditional sentence for his unnatural act was death. When the case came to Frederick's attention, he simply gave an order that set most of his subjects laughing: "Not death. Transfer him to the infantry!"

Always the quality of government was kept high. Corrupt officials, when discovered, were immediately carted off to jail, regardless of rank. Officials or servants who could give back as sarcastic an answer as the King's own caustic remarks were often rewarded or even promoted. Frederick was, of course, an absolute monarch. This meant that he did not always play the role of lovable and cranky elder statesman; for he most certinaly did not have to do so. For example, Frederick like so many men of the Enlightenment, was not a believer in traditional Christianity. Frederick the Great was a Deist, and like others of similar persuasion he was contemptuous of organized religion. Frederick offended many traditional Protestants with his mocking taunts. He would commonly ask people who had been to communion, derisively, if they had "well digested the body and blood of

Christ?" Taken together, all of these characteristics were certainly highly individualistic. Yet, he did have enough traits in common with a few others who ruled in his day to share the label "Enlightened Despot" with them. It is to a discussion of Frederick the Great's Enlightened Despotism, so much a part of his style and so lacking in the French kings, that we now turn.

* * * * * * * *

The term Enlightened Despotism presents some problems. To many people the adjective appears to contravene the noun. For them, saying Enlightened Despotism is rather like saying "clean dirt." Yet the term has stuck. The notion is based on the idea that the monarch, having studied the enlightened doctrines of eighteenth-century writers, particularly the doctrines of a group of French writers of that day called the *philosophes*, knew better than did his subjects what was good for them. The term implies that this enlightened ruler ought to have despotic powers to carry out his reforms. These reforms, in contradistinction to the traditional absolutism of the French model, were supposed to be simultaneously good for the people and to the advantage of the state.

The *philosophes*, and other enlightened writers of the eighteenth century, were harsh critics of the general style of life in society developing during previous centuries. It must be remembered that, at the end of the eighteenth century, living conditions were coarse and crude in all of Europe. Such conditions over some three centuries or so had bred into the mass of people an indifference to suffering which would now be considered quite inhuman. Most towns in Europe had whipping-posts for public floggings.

119

Bear-baiting or cock-fighting were popular
public sports. Inmates of asylums were often
exposed in cages so that visitors might poke
fun at them and tease them as if they were
animals. Death was everywhere. Given the
unsanitary conditions of the time, death carried
off every second child before it was ten years
old. Flies swarmed above open sewers and
cesspools. Bathing was a luxury in which
few indulged. The poor were unable to buy
meat and their low-protein diet meant inadequate
nourishment and resultant poor resistance
to diseases.

The *philosophes* hoped to change all
this, this coarse world of the seventeenth
century which had carried over into the
eighteen century. Their idea was to bring
about the needed changes through the reform
efforts from above in society of philosopher-
kings. Although no such ruler seemed to be
available in France, Frederick the Great of
Prussia appeared to be their theories transformed into the flesh.

Frederic gave credence to this particular
notion about him with his oft-stated motto:
"I am the first servant of the state."
Typically, when a delegation of townspeople
came to Frederick to give him their thanks
for a donation he had made to them to rebuild
part of their town, destroyed by fire, Frederick
replied: "You have no need to thank me; it
was my duty. . . ." Unlike Louis XIV, Frederick
the Great did not believe that his absolutism
rested on divine designation. Instead, in
keeping with the enlightened attitudes of
his age, Frederick believed that his authority
rested upon his ability to do better for his
people that they could do for themselves.

Frederick the Great believed that
the monarch was subject to the law. If he
expected the people to pay heavy taxes, unlike

the French monarch, he felt bound to return
to the people sizeable portions of the money
extracted from them in free gifts or projects
aimed at enhancing their general state of
well being. His reforms from above removed
the necessity of violent change from below
in the manner of that upsurge of the people
which convulsed France during the revolutionary
years of 1789-1799.

It must be remembered that Frederick's
government was benevolent toward the people
because he thought that mankind was incapable
of taking care of itself and that the few
superior individuals among all humans thus
had to see to the needs of the rest. In
private he called the people canaille and
riffraff. On one occasion some of the people
within his inner circle objected to his use
of such terminology. Frederick then answered
such criticism by saying: "Put an old monkey
on a horse and send it through the streets
and it will act the same as a common person."

It was Frederick's belief that he
was one of a few superior people that caused
him to surround himself with intellectuals
of his own calibre. It was one of his efforts
to obtain the kind of intellectual companionship he believed he should have around him
that inspired Frederick to persuade Voltaire
to move into Prussian quarters for a prolonged
stay. The death of Voltaire's most recent
mistress and Frederick's offer of 40,000 talers
in traveling money finally convinced the great
French writer to come in 1750. At first,
the two fine minds seemed to have little but
admiration for each other. Voltaire wrote
highly favorable reports of his life with
the King of Prussia back to his friends in
France. On one occasion Voltaire even wrote
glowingly to his correspondents that Frederick
was either by far the best ruler in all of
Europe "or I am the most stupid man in the

world." In time, however, the great French
wit began to quarrel with "his king." Voltaire,
used to extravagant living, continued to ask
for too much money to sustain his life style.
Finally, the somewhat avaricious man of letters
became outraged when Frederick cut his coffee
and sugar supply. Moreover, Voltaire's streak
of avarice had led him to become involved
in a lawsuit with a prominent Berlin financier.
The last straw for Frederick, however, fell
in the intellectual realm. Voltaire took
the opposite side in a quarrel between two
members of Berlin's Academy of Arts. Voltaire
finally left in a huff during March of 1753
and returned to France. The truth was that
both men were prima donnas who expected, to
some extent, that the other would rotate as
a satellite in his orbit. The two famous
figures continued to correspond until
Voltaire's death, but they never met again.
By the time that he was very old, Voltaire
had cooled enough in his anger at Frederick
to suggest that "Frederick the Great become
Frederick the Immortal!" Earlier, however,
the Enlightenment's most influential figure
had departed Prussia in a sufficiently dark
mood to publish an anonymous book suggesting
that Frederick was a homosexual whose relationships with his pages was questionable. For
his part, Frederick contemptuously dismissed
such charges.

The truth was, then, that Frederick
felt that his friendship and regard should
be given to the Voltaires of this world. He
personally had utter contempt for the common
man. But it would be naive to suggest that
a man with such a superiority complex could
not be a good king for his people. Soon after
he had come to the throne, Frederick's notion
of his obligation to serve the state set him
to working very hard through the centralized
framework established by his father. In fact,
he took even greater power into his own hands

than had Frederick William I and depended even less on the General Directory. Like his father before him, Frederick the Great gave minute personal direction to every branch of government. This fact had its advantages. Decisions by the King were far more rapid than majority votes of any board or the group decision of any set of ministries. He carried much further his father's work of educating Prussian officials to high standards of duty, honesty, efficiency, and impartial justice. The great disadvantage in all this, the criticism often made of this highly personal system of government, was much like the strictures made upon another Prussian named Otto von Bismarck a century later; in both cases the critique had it that the people involved developed a method of running the state that was unlikely to work in the hands of another person who did not equal the creator of the method in genius. Since Frederick did most of the important work himself, he had not developed ministers of outstanding ability to take over the autocratic machinery of the state by the time he left the scene.

Under Frederick the Great's guidance, in woolens, linen, porcelain, and many other items, Prussia became a strong manufacturing state. By his death, it was, although essentially still an agrarian land, the fourth manufacturing country in the world. Since his was still basically an agrarian state, Frederick did what he could to ameliorate the lot of the peasant. He did not, however, attack the institution of serfdom directly; for Junker resistance was far too great in that area. The King of Prussia did manage, however, to improve the general quality of agriculture by sending agents to England and, on their return, putting the better methods coming to use in the west into effect on his own lands. It was also Frederick II who began the systematic planting and developing of

pines and firs that eventually made Germany
into a world leader in modern methods of
forestry.

Between his wars, Frederick carried
out a program of public works, building many
prominent public buildings in Berlin. He
also reformed and codified the law. He
improved the quality of Prussian judges. As
mentioned in the previous chapter, he became
a leader in Europe in restricting the barbaric
practices of earlier ages which had become
commonplace in judicial punishments.

In sum, Frederick the Great's rule
in Prussia was the end product of the extra-
ordinary development of the Brandenburg-
Prussian state. That state had grown from
a weak electorate into the strongest and best-
run state among the Germanies even though
its population was less than that of England
and far less than that of France. Under
Frederick's rule, Prussia had become powerful
enough to rival Austria for influence over
the German states. Frederick had, in fact,
elevated Prussia to great importance among
other European powers. Through all of this
the Prussian style of absolutism, with the
almost unbelievable attention to detail
demonstrated by Frederick William I and
Frederick the Great, runs like a bright thread
through the tapestry depicting the rise of
his kingdom. Unfortunately, as it was in
all absolutist systems, whatever positive
assets rulers like these two had they could
not transmit them through hereditary to their
successors. The Prussian style of absolutism
would demonstrate its flaws after 1786, if
in a different fashion than the French did
by the arrival of their revolution in 1789.
The Prussians never had a revolution. However,
under a lesser ruler, the Prussians were
conquered by Napoleon. But in that instance
the Prussian spirit of reform from above, of

the government's duty to the people, was to
be carried forward in the face of defeat,
not by the monarch, but by state administrators
like the Freiherr vom Stein toward further
reform and it helped enhance the reinvigoration
of Prussia during the nineteenth century.

CHAPTER VII

PRUSSIANISM AND NAZISM

After the end of World War I, Adolf Hitler and his political party began their famous rise from the gutters of Munich to control over Germany. In the Nazi's scurrilous newspaper, the *Völkischer Beobachter* (The Racist Observer) it was not uncommon for an article to appear featuring the famous Prussian ruler Frederick the Great. In such articles, Frederick was transformed into something of a prototype Nazi. In refutation of these portraits of Frederick-as-Nazi, German historian Gerhard Ritter, writing after the Third Reich had crumbled into ashes, asserted that he had often implied delicately during the years of the Nazi dictatorship, as blunt assertions would probably have placed him in a concentration camp, that, instead of a comparison between Frederick the Great and Nazism, a contrast ought to have been drawn.

Ritter's view was that these two historical figures--Frederick the Great and Adolf Hitler--could be judged properly only in terms of what they actually achieved in the circumstances of their own periods in history. In Ritter's opinion, Frederick's international policy always had displayed limited objectives; Frederick wanted to obtain Silesia to strengthen his state, and then to keep Silesia, but he yearned for little more than that. Moreover, Frederick's post-1763 policy of attempting to restrain Russia points in this same general direction. For his part, Hitler's aims and aspirations in foreign policy were seemingly limitless. The Frederician state was built on religious toleration and the voluntary limitation of state activity when that activity became

harmful to the kingdom. Hitler had often
said that he meant to go far beyond anything
ever dreamed of in Prussian absolutism to
conform all of his people to the Nazi ideal.
Most importantly, the Hitlerian state had
little respect for traditional law while
Frederick's state was based on law.

Ritter's arguments emphasizing the
differences between Frederick and Hitler seem
basically sound. But Hitler and his associates
knew little of such arguments and the Führer
of Nazism had no doubt about the lineal descent
of his state. Soon after becoming Chancellor,
he proclaimed in the Garrison Church of Potsdam,
where Frederick the Great and his father lay
buried in the vault, that the Third Reich
was the legitimate descendant of the Prussian
tradition. To reinforce this tradition, to
assert that he was the natural heir to
Prussian absolutism, Hitler went to Frederick's
coffin and there, in solemn ceremony, he placed
a crown of laurel leaves on the Prussian King's
tomb.

Hitler's appeal to the memory of
Frederick the Great should be seen in perspec-
tive. The Nazi leader had no monopoly among
Germans on appealing to the symbolism provided
by the heroic figure of Frederick the Great.
Carl Goerdeler, a central figure in the internal
German resistance to Nazism, also summoned
up the same myth-symbol in quite a different
way. He wrote that Germany's salvation could
only be achieved by pursuing modest goals,
with a sense of strict economy in the spirit
of Frederick the Great. Naturally, Hitler
rejected this version of Prussianism.

In the view of some German historians,
Hitler's mistake was to follow a world view
that was the exact opposite of Frederick's;
his error was in deviating with disastrous
results from the best in old Prussian ideals

and traditions. What Frederick's feelings
about a mass lower-middle class movement like
Nazism would have been is clearly revealed
by one last Frederician quotation: "The
Enlightenment is a light from heaven for those
who stand on the heights, and a destructive
firebrand for the masses."

* * * * * * * *

If Prussian absolutism did have
influence on preparing Germany for Nazism,
it was in an indirect fashion. Prussian
absolutism conditioned an eventual German
society whose citizens tended in many cases
to subordinate their interests to the interests
of the state. Since Prussia had been
essentially an artificial creation, the work
of the Prussian army, it was basically insecure.
The army had remained the main hope for its
survival over a very long period of time.
For that reason the army, both as a means
of defense and a means of consolidating the
state territorially, decisively stamped its
seal on Prussian society. When Germany was
unified by Prussian arms through wars in 1864,
1866, and 1870-71, the Prussian stamp was
transferred to the Reich as a whole. It then
was held to be in the interest of national
security, and the German middle classes
agreed, to hold down social and economic
conflicts and achieve a synthesis of belief
along Prussian lines.

This holding to the Prussian ideal
meant that Germany did not have the revolutions
or organic changes that eventually brought
about parliamentary-democratic advancements
in France and Great Britain. And why should
Prussia, and then imperial Germany, ever have
had a French-style revolution or experienced
English-style organic reform? Prussia's
enlightened absolutism brought benefits to

its subjects which were the envy of
contemporaries abroad. There is little need
for evolution when reform is carried out from
above by enlightened edict. That practice
of reform from above was basic to the Prussian
tradition long after the death of Frederick
the Great. Perhaps the writings of the great
German author Johann Wolfgang von Goethe (1749-
1832) can illustrate this point. In 1824,
Goethe set pen to paper as follows:

> Revolutions are quite impossible so
> long as governments are always just
> and aware of what is going on in order
> that they can introduce necessary
> improvements and not resist until what
> is necessary is forced upon them from
> below. Enlightened despotism never
> occurred in France, while however great
> its faults in retrospect in Prussia and
> under Joseph II in Austria it served as
> an example to many contemporaries that
> was worthy of emulation. . . . German
> progress made through enlightened
> absolutism was ultimately the cause of
> German political underdevelopment, when
> that development is compared with that
> of nations to the west.

The old Prussian ideal really only
ceased to shape German policy after the departure
of Otto von Bismarck in 1890. Between 1890
and 1914, the simple Prussian codes of honor
and duty to the state were no longer sufficient
to cope with the complexities of the industrial
age. What remained of the old Prussia by
the beginnings of World War I could be seen
in the external trappings, the military parades,
marches and sabre rattling of William II's
German Reich. During the reign of Kaiser
William II, a German policy, imperialistic
and potentially irrational in tone, replaced
the old Prussian course of action, a course

seeking only limited ends. It was thus a
false interpretation of Prussian tradition
that Hitler inherited and falsified further.
The term "Prussian heritage" became a synonym
for the German policy of pursuing aims that
resulted in needless clashes with other powers
after 1890. This practice bore little
resemblance to the traditional Prussian system.
In this way the idea of Prussianism became
a romanticized vehicle to carry forward modern
and aggressive German nationalism. For this
reason, the Allies during World War II equated
the traditions of Prussia with Hitler's
National Socialism. Ironically, it was the
remaining core of the old Prussians, then
army officers, many of whom still believed
in honor and duty, who attempted to take
Hitler's life in July of 1944. Their failure
caused the extinction of the remnants of that
class by Hitler's representatives of the
radicalized bourgeoisie. German writer
Joachim Fest has described accurately the
final dissolution of the old Prussian honor-
bound caste in 1944 with their attempt on
Hitler's life thusly: "Rarely has a social
class made its exit from history more
impressively."

The name of Prussia still evokes
memories. It stirs both fond thoughts and
highly negative ones. But Prussia remains
for us as students of history an important
example of a state governed by an influential
variant form of absolutism, an illustration
helping us in our understanding of a governing
system that typified an era very different
than our own.

Prussia now fades into history. The
Garrison Church at Potsdam is gone.
Frederick William and Frederick the Great
have come to rest in the chapel of the
ancestral castle of the Hohenzollerns near
Stuttgart. Side by side they lie under the

worn and tattered flags of Purssian regiments. One has to listen very closely in that ancient chamber to hear the faint echoes of an army which has turned from the adornment of spiked helmets and regimental devices to the unfettered pursuit of the mark, from the Prussian tradition of quick reform from above to the practice of painstaking parliamentarianism from below.

SELECTED READINGS

Bruford, W. H. *Germany in the Eighteenth Century.*
    Cambridge: 1935.

Carsten, F. L. *The Origins of Prussia.* London:
    1954.

Catt, Henri Alexandre. *Frederick the Great: The
    Memoirs of His Reader, Henri de Catt, 1758-1760.*
    2 vols. Translated by F. S. Flint.
    London: 1916; reprint ed., Cambridge,
    Massachusetts: 1953.

Craig, Gordon A. *The Politics of the Prussian Army,
    1640-1945.* New York: 1964.

Demeter, Karl. *The German Officer Corps in Society
    and State 1650-1945.* Translated by
    Angus Malcom. London: 1965.

Dorwart, R. A. *The Administrative Reforms of
    Frederick William of Prussia.*

Duffy, C. *The Army of Frederick the Great.* London:
    1974.

Ergang, Robert. *The Potsdam Führer: Frederick
    William I, Father of Prussian Militarism.*
    New York: 1941.

Fay, Sidney B. *The Rise of Brandenberg-Prussia.*
    New York: 1937; revised: 1964.

Gaxotte, Pierre. *Frederick the Great.* New Haven:
    1942.

Gooch, George P. *Frederick the Great: The Ruler,
    The Writer, the Man.* New York: 1947.

Hatton, R. *Europe in the Age of Louis XIV.* London:
    1969.

Hatton, R. *Louis XIV and His World*. London: 1972.

Horn, David B. *Frederick the Great and the Rise of Prussia*. London: 1964.

Koch, H. W. *A History of Prussia*. London: 1978.

Macartney, C. A., ed. *The Habsburg and Hohenzollern Dynasties in the Seventeenth and Eighteenth Centuries*. London: 1970.

Nelson, Walter H. *The Berliners: Their Sage and Their City*. New York: 1969.

Ritter, Gerhard. *Frederick the Great*. 1968.

Rosenberg, Hans. *Bureaucracy, Aristocracy, and Autocracy: The Prussian Experience 1660-1815*. Cambridge, Massachusetts: 1966.

Schevill, Ferdinand. *The Great Elector*. Chicago: 1947.

Seward, D. *The Monks of War: The Military Religious Orders*. London: 1972.

Simon, Edith. *The Making of Frederick the Great*. Boston: 1963.

Temperly, Harold. *Frederick the Great and Kaiser Joseph: An Episode of War and Diplomacy in the Eighteenth Century*. 2nd ed. New York: 1968.

Wedgwood, C. V. *The Thirty Years' War*. London: 1938.